Harmony In Marriage

Becoming One in Christ

Couple's Workbook

56-Day Devotional

Robert Rodriguez

Harmony In Marriage: Couple's Workbook

Copyright © 2025 Robert Rodriguez.

All rights reserved.

ISBN: 9798320663760

Rev. 2025.02.04

All Scripture quotations, unless otherwise indicated, are taken from the Holy Bible, New International Version®, NIV®. Copyright ©1973, 1978, 1984, 2011 by Biblica, Inc.™ Used by permission of Zondervan. All rights reserved worldwide. www.zondervan.comThe "NIV" and "New International Version" are trademarks registered in the United States Patent and Trademark Office by Biblica, In

This workbook belongs to:

_____

Harmony In Marriage: Couple's Workbook

Table of Contents

INTRODUCTION ... 7
   Workbook Layout ... 8

PART ONE: HOPE ... 10
   Day 1: Finding True Hope ... 11
   Day 2: Anchoring Hope ... 14
   Day 3: Giving Hope ... 17
   Day 4: Hope Together ... 20
   Day 5: Roots of Resilience ... 24
   Day 6: Our Story of Hope ... 27
   Day 7: A Foundation of Hope ... 30

WEEK TWO: INFLUENCE ... 32
   Day 8: Power of Influence ... 33
   Day 9: Hidden Battles ... 36
   Day 10: Looking Back ... 40
   Day 11: Bonds of Unity ... 43
   Day 12: Embracing Influence ... 46
   Day 13: Being Reconcilable ... 49
   Day 14: Rooted in Love ... 52

WEEK THREE: EXPERIENTIAL FIDELITY ... 54
   Day 15: Experiential Fidelity ... 55
   Day 16: A Shared Journey ... 58
   Day 17: Growing Together ... 61
   Day 18: Delight Together ... 64
   Day 19: Silent Drift ... 67

- Day 20: Renewing Connection 70
- Day 21: Everyday Joy 73

WEEK FOUR: INTELLECTUAL FIDELITY 75

- Day 22: Intellectual Fidelity 76
- Day 23: Opening a Channel 79
- Day 24: Navigating the Storm 82
- Day 25: Learning Together 85

Day 26: Love and Respect 88

- Day 27: Intellectual Unity 91
- Day 28: A New Beginning 94

WEEK FIVE: FINANCIAL FIDELITY 96

- Day 29: Financial Fidelity 97
- Day 30: Financial Unity 100
- Day 31: Small Things 103
- Day 32: United Headship 106
- Day 33: Sharing Stewardship 109
- Day 34: Restoration 112
- Day 35: Treasured Heart 115

WEEK SIX: EMOTIONAL FIDELITY 117

- Day 36: Emotional Fidelity 118
- Day 37: Bids of Affection 121
- Day 38: With Love 124
- Day 39: True Intimacy 127
- Day 40: The Battle Within 130
- Day 41: Unrelenting Compassion 133
- Day 42: Tapestry of Grace 136

WEEK SEVEN: SEXUAL FIDELITY 138

Day 43: Sexual Fidelity 139

Day 44: A Renewed Heart 142

Day 45: Looking Forward 145

Day 46: Song of Love 148

Day 47: Healing Together 151

Day 48: Fortifying Love 154

Day 49: A Healing Journey 157

WEEK EIGHT: SPIRITUAL FIDELITY 159

Day 50: Spiritual Fidelity 160

Day 51: A Journey Back 163

Day 52: Ritual of Connection 166

Day 53: Refocusing Faith 168

Day 54: Full Armor of God 171

Day 55: Harmony In Marriage 174

Day 56: I Do 177

What's Next? 179

About The Ministry 180

About The Author 181

INTRODUCTION

This mystery is profound, and I am saying that it refers to Christ and the church.

Ephesians 5:32

Welcome to the *Harmony In Marriage Couples Workbook*, a companion to our journey through understanding and deepening the bond of marriage as outlined in the accompanying book. This workbook facilitates reading, reflection, discussion, and growth between you and your spouse as you navigate the depths of a biblical marriage.

As you work through this workbook, you are encouraged to approach each section with an open heart and mind. This is a safe space for both of you to express your thoughts, fears, hopes, and dreams. Remember, the goal is not to complete this workbook with perfect answers but to deepen your understanding and commitment to each other under God's guiding principles.

This workbook is your journey at your own pace. Still, taking at least eight weeks (assuming you follow the reading plan) is recommended to consider every module thoughtfully and intentionally. We encourage you to join a *Harmony In Marriage* class or study group and engage in Biblical Couples Counseling throughout this journey. There is no need to rush; your marriage is an invaluable gift worth all the time and effort. We strongly recommend you complete each module in order, as each does build upon the last. Regardless of how you navigate this resource, remember that you are not alone. God is with you in this journey, seeking to strengthen, heal, and bless your marriage.

We pray this becomes an invaluable guide toward building a more joyful, resilient, and Christ-centered marriage. May it inspire open, honest, and loving communication and lead you both to a deeper, more fulfilling partnership.

Harmony In Marriage: Couple's Workbook

Workbook Layout

This small group workbook is divided into 56 days over eight weeks, covering the *Harmony In Marriage* book. Each day includes one ore more of the following:

Daily Devotionals and Prayer open each day with short, inspiring passages and prayers designed to be read with your spouse before beginning your daily routine. These devotionals aim to help you both connect spiritually, take a moment to reflect, and set a positive tone for the day ahead. They prepare your minds and hearts for the reading and reflection of the day. We strongly encourage husbands to lead their wives in this prayer every morning (even if over the phone).

Daily Reading is a reading plan to help you work through *Harmony In Marriage* throughout the study. Keeping up with your spouse or small group can be daunting, so this has been designed to make it simple. While there is a summary for the reading, it is recommended to diligently read everything (most days should take you less than 20 minutes). The summaries can help refresh your memory before you begin the exercises, especially if you are going through the workbook a second or third time.

Key Points are concise summaries highlighting each day's core messages and relevant scripture. These are meant to facilitate deeper exploration and understanding of the material covered. Each of these has one or more relevant Bible verses associated with them. While you might begin to see patterns (the same verses day to day, week to week), that is intentional, and it is essential to read them. We suggest reading them alone and together during your daily reflection time. Journal these verses and put them up around your home; these are the Word of God that should be written on your hearts.

Personal Reflection Prompts are designed to help you process your experiences and emotions considering your walk with Christ. These prompts invite you to examine your heart and consider the personal changes God calls you to make. By using 'I' statements, you focus on your relationship with Jesus, seeking His guidance and conviction. This is not a space to criticize or vent about others but an opportunity to bring your fears, frustrations, and sins before the Lord and your spouse in humble confession and seek forgiveness in humility and repentance. Sharing these reflections with your spouse fosters vulnerability and demonstrates the biblical confession essential for building genuine intimacy and unity in marriage.

⚭ **Couple's Discussion** prompts provide profound discussion opportunities regarding your marriage and the changes you agree to make as a husband or wife. It would be best to journal these discussions from your perspective, making both 'I' and 'we' statements when possible. This is an opportunity to assess your communication, get on the same page, and celebrate each other. We recommend you come together after completing these for discussion and sharing. Consider these an extension of your marriage covenant, but always carefully consider where you are placing your hope and expectations (Jesus and not your spouse), and allow His grace to bless both of you continuously.

👫 **Fidelity Builders** provides opportunities to practice what you learn throughout the week. These should not be considered optional. Make every effort to dive into these with enthusiasm and expectations of learning about yourself, your spouse, and God.

PART ONE: HOPE

Day 1: Finding True Hope

Not only so, but we also glory in our sufferings, because we know that suffering produces perseverance; perseverance, character; and character, hope.

Romans 5:3-4

In marriage and life, we all experience moments of longing—yearning for something deeper and more meaningful. That longing often points to our need for hope. True hope is not just wishing things would improve; it is steady and unshakable, rooted in God's promises.

Think about Adam and Eve. When sin entered their story, it separated them from God, leaving an emptiness. We can relate. How often do we try to fill that emptiness with achievements, relationships, or distractions like social media, shopping, or perhaps even ministry? But those are only temporary fixes. In marriage, this search for hope is even more critical. Challenges can leave us feeling lost, but Christ's hope anchors us. It shifts our focus from the struggles to God, who offers light and strength. Let Christ's hope steady your marriage, guide you through tough times, and remind you that you are never alone.

Prayer

Lord,

Fill our hearts with Your true hope. Help us to seek You first, above all else, and to anchor our marriage in Your eternal promises. Teach us to trust in Your faithfulness and to overflow with the joy and peace that come from Your Spirit. In moments of doubt or despair, remind us that our hope in You is never in vain.

Amen.

Read: Chapter 1, Pages 19-34

This section from "Our Need for Hope" in *Harmony In Marriage* discusses the multifaceted nature of hope, its origins, and its importance, particularly in the context of marriage. It explores how hope is foundational to overcoming life's challenges and is essential for building resilience and mental strength. We also explore the story of Dylan and Sarah, illustrating how personal backgrounds and external pursuits can create barriers to genuine hope and intimacy within a marriage. The text emphasizes that true hope, especially biblical, is rooted in a relationship with Christ rather than worldly or temporary solutions.

🔑 Key Points

- **Hope as a Fundamental Human Need (Romans 5:3-4)**

  Hope is essential for overcoming challenges and sustaining mental and emotional well-being.

- **The Sinful Origin of Hope and Redemption (Genesis 3:15)**

  Sin disrupted the perfect relationship between humanity and God, creating a deep yearning for reconciliation and hope fulfilled in Christ.

- **The Role of Hope in Marriage (Ephesians 5:25)**

  In marriage, hope is crucial for navigating challenges and is anchored in the belief in Christ's redeeming.

- **The Dangers of Misplaced Hope (Matthew 6:21)**

  Placing hope in temporary, worldly things or the wrong aspect of a relationship leads to disappointment and a void that only God can fill.

- **The Path to True Hope (Psalm 62:5)**

  True hope is found in a relationship with God and is essential for enduring happiness and fulfillment, particularly within the marriage covenant.

✒ Personal Reflection

Think about a time when you leaned on something temporary—like a job, possessions, or someone's approval—to find fulfillment. How did you feel when it fell short of what you really needed? Now, think about a moment when you trusted God's promises instead. How did that change your perspective or give you peace?

_____

_____

_____

_____

_____

_____

_____

⚭ Couple's Discussion

Together, recall a challenging or disappointing situation you faced in your marriage. Share how each of you responded during that time. Were there moments when you leaned on each other and God, or did you seek comfort elsewhere? Confess any fears, frustrations, or struggles you experienced before God together, and discuss how trusting in Christ might have strengthened you then or how it can guide you through future challenges.

Day 2: Anchoring Hope

May the God of hope fill you with all joy and peace as you trust in Him, so that you may overflow with hope by the power of the Holy Spirit.

Romans 15:13

Life can feel like a vast ocean, with our souls sometimes drifting in waves of uncertainty and storms of conflict, especially within marriage. Yet, a firm, steadfast, and unshakable anchor is available to us: Hope in God. This hope is not just wishful thinking but a confident expectation rooted in God's promises, upheld by His faithfulness, and energized by the Holy Spirit. It brings joy and peace, even in the middle of trials. Dylan and Sarah's story reminds us of this truth. They struggled, each seeking comfort in the wrong places. But when they turned back to Christ, they found their anchor. True hope was not in external validation or personal success but in the transformative power of God's love and grace.

Daily Prayer

Lord,

You are the God of hope. Fill our hearts with Your joy and peace as we trust in You. Help us anchor our marriage in Your promises and overflow with the hope from Your Holy Spirit. Teach us to lean on You in times of trouble and celebrate Your presence in times of joy. May our relationship reflect Your love and be a testament to the enduring hope we have in You.

Amen.

Read: Chapter 1, Pages 35-39

The end of Chapter 1 discusses the pitfalls of prideful hope in marriage, using Dylan and Sarah's story as an example. Their misplaced hope and pride led to resentment and a communication breakdown. The chapter emphasizes that idolatry and self-reliance can distort the essence of marriage, which should reflect Christ's relationship with the Church. Couples are encouraged to redirect their relationship towards God, recognizing that genuine hope and love can heal and restore.

🔑 Key Points

- **Prideful Hope Leads to Marital Discord (Proverbs 13:10)**

  Pride and misplaced hope can create barriers in communication and understanding within a marriage.

- **Idolatry Deteriorates Marital Unity (Exodus 20:3)**

  Placing anything above God, including your marriage and spouse, leads to dissatisfaction a lack of fulfillment, and suffering.

🪶 Personal Reflection

Take a moment to think about anything that might have taken priority over your relationship with your spouse or God— possessions, achievements, recognition, or even the idea of a perfect marriage. What steps can you take to refocus and keep God at the center of your marriage?

_____
_____
_____
_____
_____
_____
_____

📖 Read: Chapter 2, Pages 40-48

Chapter 2 asserts that the Bible is a powerful source of hope, teaching through stories of endurance and encouragement. Couples are urged to immerse themselves in Scripture, not for quick fixes but for transformative insights that apply to life and marriage. The chapter illustrates how biblical narratives provide hope and guidance, emphasizing the importance of God's promises, redemption through Christ, and the power of faith and endurance.

🔑 Key Points

- **Scripture Teaches and Provides Hope (Romans 15:4)**

  The Bible is a tool for learning and finding hope through God's promises and the endurance of its characters.

- **Hope in God's Promises (2 Peter 1:4)**

Believers are encouraged to trust God's promises for guidance and support in marriage.

- **Redemption and Salvation through Christ (John 3:16)**
  The hope of redemption and eternal life is central to Christian faith and marriage.

- **Examples of Faith and Perseverance (Hebrews 11:1)**
  Biblical stories of Abraham, Hannah, and Ruth show how faith and hope in God can overcome life's challenges.

- **The Bible as a Guide for Marriage (Psalm 119:105)**
  Couples are encouraged to use the Bible as a guide to strengthen their relationship and find hope in God's teachings.

🪶 Personal Reflection

Think back to a time when you and your spouse faced a significant challenge in your marriage. Did you truly seek God's wisdom and peace during that season, or were you focused on finding a quick solution? Reflect on whether you allowed His Word to deeply shape your heart and actions or if you rushed past the opportunity for transformation. How can you approach Scripture differently moving forward, inviting God's truth to renew your perspective and bring healing and unity to your marriage?

_____
_____
_____
_____
_____
_____

💍 Couple's Discussion

Share with your spouse a biblical story or promise that has inspired hope during difficult times. As you reflect on this, open up about how it has personally shaped your faith and trust in God. Confess before God any fears, frustrations, or doubts you've faced during those moments, and invite your spouse to do the same. Discuss how this shared biblical truth can not only guide you through current or future challenges but also strengthen the foundation of trust and intimacy in your marriage.

Harmony In Marriage: Couple's Workbook

Day 3: Giving Hope

Therefore encourage one another and build each other up, just as in fact you are doing.

1 Thessalonians 5:11

Marriage is a journey where encouragement becomes a soothing balm, helping heal wounds and strengthen bonds. Today, let us focus on the power of lifting one another. It is a divine calling that can transform our relationships and reflect God's love. In the busyness of life, we often overlook how much impact a kind word, a supportive gesture, or simply listening can have. Yet, Scripture reminds us that encouragement can lift the human spirit.

The Apostle Paul knew the early Christians' struggles and stressed the importance of mutual encouragement. This is just as vital in marriage. Encouragement is not about shallow compliments or praise but about truly affirming your spouse's worth, efforts, and heart. It means seeing them as God sees them and reminding them of His love and promises, especially in moments of doubt or struggle.

📖 Daily Prayer

Heavenly Father,

We thank You for the gift of my spouse and the journey we share. Help me to be a source of encouragement, reflecting Your love and compassion. Please grant me the wisdom to see my partner's needs and the words to uplift their spirit. May our relationship be a testament to Your grace as we encourage and build each other up in Your love.

Amen.

👫 Fidelity Builder: A Letter of Encouragement

Today, write a letter of encouragement to your spouse. Begin by praying for guidance, asking God to help you express your thoughts and feelings in a way that will uplift and strengthen your partner. In your letter, be specific about the qualities you admire in them and the ways they have positively impacted your life. Remind them of God's love and the promises in His Word that pertain to their current challenges. Let them know you are there for them, committed to supporting and encouraging them in all circumstances.

1. **Reflect Before Writing**

    Before writing, spend a few moments in quiet reflection and prayer. Think about your partner's qualities, the journey you have shared, the challenges you have overcome, and your dreams for the future. Consider the aspects of your relationship that fill you with gratitude.

2. **Start with Affection**

    Begin your letter with a term of endearment and an expression of your love. This sets a positive, loving tone for the rest of the message.

3. **Express Gratitude**

    Detail the specific qualities in your partner for which you are grateful. Acknowledge the everyday acts of kindness, moments of strength, or gestures of love they have shown. Be specific – this personal recognition is incredibly affirming.

4. **Highlight Their Strengths**

    Identify and praise your partner's strengths. This could be their patience, sense of humor, resilience, creativity, or other attributes you admire. Explain how these qualities have positively impacted you and your relationship.

5. **Share Encouraging Words**

    Offer encouragement, especially if your partner is facing challenges or doubts. Remind them of their capabilities and past successes. Show your unwavering support and belief in their ability to overcome obstacles.

6. **Reaffirm Your Commitment**

    Reiterate your commitment to your relationship and to facing life's challenges together. Emphasize the strength of your partnership and your readiness to support each other through thick and thin.

7. **Recall Shared Memories**

    Bring up happy or meaningful memories you have shared, especially those demonstrating your growth as a couple or where you have successfully worked through difficulties together.

8. **End with Hope and Love**

    Conclude your letter with expressions of hope for the future and reaffirmation of your love. You might include a quote, a line of poetry, or a personal message that resonates with your relationship.

9. **Present the Letter**

   Decide how you want to present the letter. You might choose a special occasion or a moment when your partner could use a boost. Alternatively, leaving the letter as a surprise for them to find can add an element of spontaneity and delight.

10. **Create a Tradition**

    Consider making this an ongoing tradition. You could write letters on anniversaries, after significant life events, or anytime you feel moved to express your love and gratitude. This practice can become a cherished part of your relationship, creating a collection of love letters that document your journey together.

11. **Respond and Reflect**

    Encourage your partner to respond, whether in writing or through conversation. This can open deeper communication and provide further insight into each other's thoughts and feelings.

Letters of encouragement are a powerful tool in building and sustaining a strong, hopeful relationship. They are tangible reminders of your love, support, and shared dreams, providing comfort and inspiration in joyful and challenging times.

Day 4: Hope Together

Yes, my soul, find rest in God;
my hope comes from him.

Psalm 62:5

God's Word is not just text on a page—it is alive, active, and capable of transforming our hearts and minds. Engaging deeply with Scripture plants seeds of hope, helping us grow and see life in new ways. This connection allows us to view each other and our circumstances through God's eyes, turning resentment into grace and suspicion into trust.

But understanding Scripture is just the beginning. We also need to closely examine the external factors that might be draining our hope. Are our social media habits, workplace environments, or friendships aligned with God's love, mercy, and faithfulness teachings? Or are they sources of discouragement?

Building a sanctuary of hope takes more than reflection—it requires intentional action. It means setting boundaries against negative influences and fostering relationships that encourage spiritual growth. When we align our environment with Christ-centered priorities, we create a sanctuary of hope that extends beyond our home and into every part of our lives.

Daily Prayer

Lord,

Help us to build a sanctuary of hope within our marriage, rooted in Your Word and shielded from the world's distractions. Teach us to discern and eliminate the negative influences in our lives and to embrace the practices that draw us closer to You. May our home, relationships, and daily activities reflect Your love and hope.

Amen.

Read: Chapter 2, Pages 48-56

Dylan and Sarah's journey through Scripture transformed their marriage and lives, illustrating the profound impact of God's Word. By internalizing and living out the truths found in the Bible, they replaced counterfeit hopes with genuine hope, leading to significant positive changes. This narrative serves as a testament to the power of Scripture to transform lives and marriages, offering hope and guidance through God's eternal truths.

🗝 Key Points

- **Transformation Through Scripture (Hebrews 4:12)**

    Dylan and Sarah experienced a profound transformation in their marriage by actively engaging with Scripture. They discovered that the Bible was not just text but a living entity that changed their perspectives and behaviors.

- **Viewing Each Other Through God's Eyes (Galatians 5:22-23)**

    As they delved deeper into the Scriptures, Dylan and Sarah began to see each other as beloved children of God, leading to grace replacing resentment and trust taking over suspicion.

- **Impact Beyond Marriage (Matthew 5:16)**

    The couple's engagement with Scripture also positively affected their interactions outside their marriage, demonstrating the transformative power of God's Word in all areas of life.

- **The Power of God's Promises (2 Peter 1:4)**

    Dylan and Sarah learned to replace counterfeit hopes with the genuine hope found in God's promises, understanding that these promises are not just comforting words but immutable truths.

- **Practical Application of Hope (Joshua 1:8)**

    The couple implemented practical steps to reinforce their hope in God, such as setting aside time for Bible study, using daily affirmations based on Scripture, and sharing testimonies of God's faithfulness.

🪶 Personal Reflection

Reflect on areas in your life and marriage where you might place unrealistic expectations on your spouse. Are there ways to shift those expectations to align more with Christ's example of love and grace? Remember that you and your spouse are works in progress, growing under God's transforming hand. How can embracing this truth help you show more incredible patience, understanding, and compassion in your relationship?

_____

_____

_____

_____

📖 Read: Chapter 3, Pages 57-61

Dylan and Sarah learn that building a marriage based on hope requires more than just understanding Scripture; it involves actively creating an environment that fosters this hope. They identify and reduce negative influences, such as social media comparison and workplace competition, aligning their actions more closely with biblical teachings. They also cultivate relationships supporting their spiritual growth, extending the sanctuary of hope beyond their personal space into every aspect of their lives.

🔑 Key Points

- **Active Engagement with Scripture (Hebrews 4:12)**

    They realize that engaging actively with Scripture transforms their perspective and behavior.

- **Contentment and Avoidance of Comparison (Philippians 4:11-13)**

    Sarah learns to find contentment by avoiding social media comparisons, aligning with teachings that caution against envy and discontent.

- **Work as Service to God (Colossians 3:23)**

    Dylan reshapes his view of work as a service to God rather than a means to personal success.

- **Fostering Positive Relationships (Proverbs 27:17)**

    They prioritize relationships that encourage their faith and marriage.

- **Transforming Their Environment (Romans 12:2)**

    By altering their environment to reflect their faith, they create a life that consistently nurtures hope.

🪶 Personal Reflection

Reflect deeply on your daily routines and the environments you are immersed in. Are there habits, such as how you engage with social media or the atmosphere at work, that you need to confess as sources of discouragement, distraction, or misplaced focus? Bring these areas before God, acknowledging where they may drain your hope, joy, or contentment. Consider how embracing biblical principles can transform these aspects of your life, allowing them to become spaces where God's truth encourages, renews, and grows you in Christ.

_____
_____
_____
_____
_____
_____
_____

⌬ Couple's Discussion

Together, list the external pressures and influences that have impacted your marriage. As you share, confess before God any fears, frustrations, or struggles these pressures have caused. Discuss how you can work together to create a 'sanctuary of hope' in your home by aligning your thoughts, actions, and relationship with God's Word and principles. Be vulnerable about what you each need from the other to make your marriage a refuge of love and faith.

Day 5: Roots of Resilience

"But blessed is the one who trusts in the Lord,
whose confidence is in him.
⁸ They will be like a tree planted by the water
that sends out its roots by the stream.
It does not fear when heat comes;
its leaves are always green.
It has no worries in a year of drought
and never fails to bear fruit."

Jeremiah 17:7-8

Marriage is not just about getting through life together; it is about growing together and building something meaningful—a place of hope and strength that can withstand whatever life throws your way. This idea of a 'Sanctuary of Hope' is about creating a marriage that goes beyond surface-level commitment and taps into a deeper spiritual connection. It is about walking together on a shared path, guided by God's wisdom and love.

In Ephesians 5, Paul talks about the importance of loving and submitting to one another out of reverence for Christ. This kind of mutual submission is not about giving up who you are. Instead, it is about lifting each other up so you can both grow into who God is calling you to be. It is about creating a relationship where you both feel understood, valued, and loved—not just by each other but in the way Christ loves His Church.

📖 Daily Prayer

Heavenly Father,

Guide us as we build our marriage into a sanctuary of hope. Help us to see each other as You see us, to love as You love, and to forgive as You forgive. May our relationship reflect Your grace and truth, becoming a beacon of hope and a testament to Your enduring love, in Jesus' name.

Amen.

📖 Read: Chapter 3, Pages 61-73

This section explores transforming marriage into a spiritual sanctuary grounded in faith and mutual understanding. It emphasizes the importance of creating a safe, nurturing environment where both individuals can grow spiritually and emotionally. The chapter highlights the pillars of prayer, empathy, forgiveness, and shared values, enabling couples to navigate life's complexities with grace and resilience. By doing so, the marriage evolves into a true sanctuary of hope, where the presence of God's love is palpable, enriching their journey together.

🔑 Key Points

- **Beyond Surface Commitment (James 2:26)**

  The chapter emphasizes that genuine marital commitment goes beyond enduring tough times like a demanding job or a rough patch with a friend. It should be rooted in a deeper spiritual connection, reflecting the sacred bond of marriage as intended by God. This is akin to the biblical concept where faith without works is dead, suggesting that hope and commitment in marriage must also be active and spiritually alive.

- **Addressing External Influences (Philippians 4:8, Colossians 3:23)**

  Recognizing and mitigating external pressures and influences is crucial. This includes societal expectations, social media comparisons, and workplace culture, which can all contribute to disillusionment and stress in a marriage. The Bible advises focusing on what is true and noble and working heartily for the Lord. It guides spouses to seek fulfillment and validation through their faith and each other rather than external accolades or societal standards.

- **Embracing Forgiveness and Empathy (Galatians 6:2)**

  Forgiveness and empathy are highlighted as essential components of a hopeful and resilient marriage. Just as Christ forgives and empathizes with us, spouses are encouraged to extend the same grace and understanding, bearing each other's burdens, and fostering an environment of healing and mutual support.

- **Transformative Power of Hope (Romans 15:13)**

  Finally, the chapter discusses the transformative power of hope in a marriage. By anchoring their relationship in God's promises and maintaining a hopeful outlook, couples can navigate challenges more effectively and build a stronger, more fulfilling union. This hope is not passive but an active trust in God's sovereignty and faithfulness, which sustains the marriage through trials and enriches the couple's spiritual journey together.

Personal Reflection

Reflect on the outside pressures or challenges that may be affecting your marriage. Confess how these influences might weaken your faith or the spiritual bond you share with your spouse. Acknowledge how you have allowed these pressures to distract you from God's promises and truth. Seek His guidance to protect your marriage by grounding it in His Word and leaning into His grace. What intentional steps can you take to refocus on God's faithfulness and nurture a deeper spiritual connection with your spouse?

_____
_____
_____
_____
_____
_____
_____
_____

⌘ Couple's Discussion

Take time together to discuss what it means for your marriage to be a 'sanctuary of hope.' Share insights from your earlier reflections and open up about your individual hopes, fears, and struggles. Be vulnerable with one another and confess before God the areas where you feel spiritually or emotionally weak. Explore practical ways to invite God's presence into your daily life and discuss how you can support each other in handling outside pressures with faith, unity, and love.

Day 6: Our Story of Hope

And let us consider how we may spur one another on toward love and good deeds, ^{25} *not giving up meeting together, as some are in the habit of doing, but encouraging one another—and all the more as you see the Day approaching.*

Hebrews 10:24-25

Marriage has its ups and downs, and every couple longs for a safe place to feel supported and understood. A 'Refuge of Hope' encourages us to see marriage as a spiritual partnership strengthened by connection to a church community. Marriage is more than daily routines—it is a covenant that mirrors Christ's relationship with the Church.

How do we build that kind of connection? By staying engaged with biblical principles and actively participating in the life of the church. The church is not just a Sunday destination but a community where we find encouragement, wisdom, and fellowship. It is where couples can grow together, find healing for past struggles, and hope for the future.

Getting involved means more than attending; it is about being vulnerable and learning together. Within this space, God's love transforms struggles into stories of faithfulness and strength.

📖 Daily Prayer

Heavenly Father,

Thank You for the gift of marriage and the church community where we can grow and flourish together. Help us to see our marriage as a spiritual journey, deeply connected to our life in the church. Teach us to lean on fellow believers' support and wisdom, find healing in Your word, and offer others hope through our testimony. May our marriage be a refuge of hope for us and all who witness Your work in our lives.

Amen.

📖 Read: Chapter 4, Pages 74-86

The chapter "Refuge of Hope" emphasizes the importance of elevating marriage from a social contract to a spiritual refuge. It stresses the profound, spiritual bond that should exist between spouses. This requires a dynamic experience of biblical principles nurtured within the church community. The church plays a crucial role in supporting and enriching the marital bond, making the marriage a true refuge of hope grounded in the shared pursuit of spiritual growth and divine purpose. To achieve this, couples must deeply integrate faith into their marital relationship. They can do this by turning to prayer, communal support, and spiritual guidance as fundamental tools for resolving conflicts, enhancing communication, and fostering a deeper connection. Active participation in church life can help couples explore, understand, and embody the divine blueprint for marriage. This approach shifts the focus from individual efforts to a collective, faith-driven journey, where the church community acts as a vital, active framework.

🗝 Key Points

- **Community Support and Spiritual Growth (Hebrews 10:24-25)**
  The church provides a nurturing environment for couples to grow spiritually and find support among fellow believers. This community helps couples navigate marriage's complexities with wisdom and grace rooted in shared faith and values.

- **Biblical Counseling and Soul Care (2 Timothy 3:16-17)**
  Guidance from church leaders and biblical counseling helps couples understand the divine purpose of marriage, emphasizing the importance of grace, forgiveness, and God's role in their union. This approach fosters a deeper spiritual connection and mutual growth.

- **Shared Service and Purpose (1 Peter 4:10)**
  Serving together in the church fosters unity and shared purpose among couples, bridging gaps in their relationship and creating a sense of partnership in a larger mission. This shared service strengthens their bond and aligns their marriage with God's work.

- **Transformation Through Faith (Romans 12:2)**
  The church's influence leads to personal and relational transformation as couples apply their spiritual gifts and redirect their energies toward ministry and community building. This change reflects the transformative power of faith in their lives and marriage. (Romans 12:2)

- **Hope and Healing (2 Corinthians 1:3-4)**

The church acts as a sanctuary where couples can find hope and healing. By engaging with the church community, couples experience the restorative power of God's love, which redefines their marriage and turns their past pains into powerful testimonies of redemption.

🪶 Personal Reflection

Reflect on the last significant challenge or conflict you faced in your marriage. Bring before God any ways you may have neglected or embraced the support of your church community during that time. Did you seek prayer, guidance, or encouragement from others in the body of Christ, or did you try to face it on your own? Confess where pride or fear may have held you back, and thank God for using His people to sustain you. Consider how you can lean more fully on your church community in the future, trusting God's design for His church to strengthen and support your marriage.

_____
_____
_____
_____
_____
_____
_____

💍 Couple's Discussion

Discuss with your spouse how your faith and involvement in your church community have shaped your marriage. Share specific moments when your church family provided support, guidance, or encouragement that strengthened your relationship. Be honest about any ways you may have struggled to integrate faith into your marriage, and together, explore how you can draw more from your church life to build a stronger bond and face future challenges with unity and trust in God.

Day 7: A Foundation of Hope

For no one can lay any foundation other than the one already laid, which is Jesus Christ.

1 Corinthians 3:11

A strong marriage, like a well-built home, requires a solid foundation. Without it, even the most beautiful structure will eventually crumble under pressure. Shifting emotions, difficult seasons, and external challenges can shake a relationship, but when a marriage is built on the firm foundation of Christ, it stands secure.

Hope in Christ is not a fragile wish but a confident expectation grounded in His unchanging character and promises. Just as a house depends on a sturdy foundation to withstand storms, a marriage rooted in the hope of Christ can endure hardships and emerge stronger. When trials come, His presence provides stability. When conflict arises, His grace offers restoration. When uncertainty threatens, His faithfulness brings peace.

You build your marriage daily—brick by brick, choice by choice. Will you build on shifting sands of personal effort and worldly wisdom, or will you establish your relationship on the unwavering foundation of Christ? When hope in Him is your cornerstone, your marriage is protected and flourishes, reflecting His love and faithfulness.

Take time today to evaluate the foundation of your marriage. Are there areas where you have relied on temporary support rather than the firm foundation of Christ? Pray together, asking God to deepen your trust in Him and strengthen the steady hope of your marriage. A home built on the foundation of Christ's hope will endure and become a testimony of His goodness and faithfulness.

📖 Daily Prayer

Heavenly Father,

Thank You for the gift of hope, a firm foundation upon which we can build our lives and marriage. Help us place our trust in You and let this hope steady us in times of trial. Strengthen our marriage with faith in Your promises and the assurance of Your love and grace. May our relationship reflect Your presence, always pointing to our eternal hope in Christ.

Amen.

🪶 Personal Reflection

Think about the times when maintaining hope in your relationship felt incredibly challenging. What were the circumstances, and what, if anything, helped you begin to regain a sense of hope? Reflect on whether prayer, scripture, or support from others played a role or if those resources were not part of your approach. How might exploring these practices, even in small steps, help you find strength and clarity as you face future challenges?

_____
_____
_____
_____
_____
_____
_____
_____

💍 Couple's Discussion

Reflect together on your first week exploring the concept of Hope and how it has shaped or reshaped your understanding of marriage. Share specific moments from the past week where you felt hope either challenged or strengthened. Be open about any fears, frustrations, or doubts, and confess these before God together. Discuss practical ways to commit to fostering a hopeful outlook in your marriage, grounded in God's promises, as you continue this journey toward harmony.

WEEK TWO: INFLUENCE

Day 8: Power of Influence

God blessed them and said to them, "Be fruitful and increase in number; fill the earth and subdue it. Rule over the fish in the sea and the birds in the sky and over every living creature that moves on the ground."

Genesis 1:28

God has entrusted us with the gift of influence, allowing us to shape the world and those around us. Genesis 1:28 shows this responsibility, while Genesis 3 reminds us of the consequences when influence is misused. This calls for discernment and alignment with God's principles—love, service, justice, and humility.

In marriage and community, our influence should reflect Christ's love, fostering unity and growth. Ephesians 5:32 reminds us that marriage reflects Christ's relationship with the Church, showing how godly influence can bring hope and transformation.

Take time today to think about how you use your influence. Are your actions and words drawing others closer to God's truth? Commit to using your influence for His glory, reflecting His heart in all you do. Let your life be a light that points others to His hope and guidance.

📖 Daily Prayer

Heavenly Father,

Thank You for the gift of influence. Help us use it wisely, aligning our actions and words with Your will. Grant us discernment to avoid selfishness and teach us to steward our influence in a way that honors You and fosters healthy relationships. May our lives reflect Christ's love and humility, drawing others to Your truth and grace, in Jesus' name.

Amen.

📖 Read: Chapter 5, Pages 90-103

In "Dangerous Influence," the chapter examines influence from a biblical standpoint, emphasizing its significant role in human interactions and its potential for positive and negative outcomes. The text highlights that while influence can be a tool for good, guiding others towards God's purpose, it can also lead to destructive paths, as illustrated by the fall of Adam and Eve due to the serpent's deceit in Genesis 3. The chapter urges individuals to recognize their capacity for influence and to wield it through love and service rather than fear and manipulation, aligning actions with God's commands for stewardship and care. It underscores the importance of using influence responsibly within society, relationships, and personal growth, always guided by biblical principles and God's ultimate plan for humanity.

🔑 Key Points

- **Inherent Nature of Influence (Genesis 1:29)**
  Influence is identified as an inherent human trait deeply embedded in our creation, allowing individuals to impact others' actions, opinions, or decisions. This concept is supported by the biblical command in Genesis 1:28, where humans are instructed to subdue the earth and have dominion, reflecting the divine mandate to use influence responsibly and for God's purposes.

- **Dual Nature of Influence (Genesis 3)**
  The text highlights the dual nature of influence, which can be used for good or evil. This is exemplified in the biblical narrative of Genesis 3, where the serpent uses influence to deceive Eve, leading to the fall of humanity. This story underscores the critical need for discernment and aligning our influence with God's will rather than succumbing to manipulative or selfish uses.

- **Stewardship and Responsibility**
  The concept of stewardship is central to the text, emphasizing that influence should be exercised as part of our God-given responsibility to care for the world and each other. This aligns with biblical teachings on stewardship and the importance of managing our resources, relationships, and the environment in a way that honors God and serves the common good.

- **Impact of Misused Influence**
  The dangers of unchecked influence are discussed, noting how it can lead to conflicts, exploitation, and moral dilemmas. The narrative points out that our influence has been tainted by sin, as illustrated by Adam and Eve's fall, highlighting the importance of ethical behavior, self-awareness, and living according to biblical values of love, justice, and humility.

- **Role of Influence in Community and Relationships (Ephesians 5:32)**
  Finally, the text explores the role of influence in fostering relationships and community, particularly within the context of the church and marriage. It suggests that when aligned with God's design, influence

can strengthen bonds, encourage mutual growth, and advance the Kingdom of God. This is supported by Ephesians 5:32, which speaks to the mystery of Christ's love for the church mirrored in the marriage union, showcasing how godly influence can illuminate the world with hope and transformation.

Personal Reflection

Consider the current influences in your life and marriage—things like TV, social media, finances, family, or even your church community. How are these influences shaping your actions and words? Are they motivated more by love and service or by fear and control? Reflect on specific situations where these influences played a role and consider whether your responses align with the idea of stewardship and love found in Genesis 1:28. How might you begin to approach these influences differently to better reflect God's design for love and care in your life and marriage?

_____
_____
_____
_____
_____
_____
_____
_____
_____
_____

Couple's Discussion

Discuss together how you can use your influence within your marriage and community to reflect God's love and purpose. Share any areas in your relationship where the misuse of influence has caused tension or conflict, and confess these struggles before God. Talk about how you can address these issues by aligning your actions with biblical principles of love, justice, and humility, and commit to supporting each other in this pursuit.

Day 9: Hidden Battles

For our struggle is not against flesh and blood, but against the rulers, against the authorities, against the powers of this dark world and against the spiritual forces of evil in the heavenly realms.

Ephesians 6:12

Genesis 3 gives us a powerful reminder of how subtle temptation and negative influences can affect marriage. The serpent's approach to Eve, bypassing Adam, highlights how division can creep into relationships, exploiting vulnerabilities and misunderstandings.

In our marriages, these influences might look like unresolved disagreements, external friendships undermining trust, or being swayed by voices not aligning with shared values. This story urges us to stay vigilant and united, guarding our relationship against anything that could lead to division.

The good news is that bringing struggles to light can lead to healing and growth. Instead of accusations, approach challenges with a heart for understanding and reconciliation. Inviting Christ into your marriage replaces deception with love, trust, and respect. This builds a strong foundation, creating a bond that can withstand external pressures and thrive in unity.

📖 Daily Prayer

Heavenly Father,

Guide us to recognize the subtle influences that threaten our marital unity. Grant us the wisdom to discern and the strength to confront these challenges with grace and love. Help us to foster an environment of transparency and trust in our relationship, always seeking to honor You and each other. May Your influence be the cornerstone of our marriage, guiding us toward a bond that reflects Your love and purity, in Jesus' Name.

Amen.

📖 Read: Chapter 5, Pages 103-105

Influence, shaped by our quest for stability and recognition, often leads us away from our spiritual roots. Authentic influence stems from aligning with core values like kindness, humility, and service, reflecting a more profound reflection of Jesus rather than personal ambition. By adopting these values, we shift from self-centered actions to fostering genuine connections and Christ-centered community. This approach redirects our personal paths and heals and strengthens relationships, creating a more meaningful and balanced life grounded in values that surpass individual desires.

🔑 Key Points

- **The Misguided Pursuit of Influence (Genesis 11)**

  Scripture illustrates humanity's misguided attempt to assert influence and secure its legacy through constructing the Tower of Babel, driven by desires for security and significance. This biblical example cautions against the dangers of pursuing influence for selfish gains, reminding us that true security and significance cannot be achieved through human efforts alone.

- **The Transformative Power of God's Presence (James 4:8)**

  James 4:8 encourages believers to "Draw near to God, and He will draw near to you." This verse underscores the transformative power of prioritizing God's presence over worldly influence. By aligning our desires with God's will, we shift from exerting control to moving in rhythms of grace, truth, and love, allowing our influence to reflect God's character and kingdom.

- **Surrender and Authentic Influence**

  The true essence of influence is not in manipulation or control but in surrendering to God's guidance and allowing His presence to shape our lives and relationships. This surrender leads to authentic influence, characterized by actions and decisions that reflect God's love, justice, and humility, ultimately impacting others positively and aligning with His divine purposes.

✒ Personal Reflection

Reflect on the areas in your marriage where you seek control or significance. How have these desires impacted your relationship with your spouse? Consider whether you are looking to worldly achievements or personal expectations to find security and importance, instead of grounding your marriage in Christ. How might shifting your focus to make Jesus the center of your marriage transform your actions and decisions, allowing you to love your spouse with grace, truth, and selflessness as Christ commands?

_____

_____

_____
_____
_____
_____
_____
_____
_____
_____

📖 Read: Chapter 6, Pages 106-113

In "Breaking Bad Influence," the narrative delves into the complexities of influence within marriage, particularly how negative influences can undermine the relationship. The chapter uses the story of Genesis 3 to illustrate how subtle and deceptive influences, like those from external friendships or internal struggles, can create discord and distance between spouses. It emphasizes the importance of discernment and unity in marriage to resist harmful influences. The chapter also discusses the necessity of exposing hidden issues to the light, acknowledging that true healing and strength in marriage come from a deep, shared commitment to Christ's teachings and guidance.

🔑 Key Points

- **Subtlety of Temptation (Genesis 3)**

  Returning to Genesis 3, we reiterate the subtlety of temptation and its potential to disrupt marital unity. Couples must remain vigilant against subtle negative influences that can enter their relationship, emphasizing the need for spiritual discernment and mutual support.

- **Importance of Discernment (Proverbs 4:23)**

  Proverbs 4:23 advises guarding one's heart, underscoring the need for relationship discernment. Spouses should be mindful of each other's concerns about external influences and seek wisdom in distinguishing between beneficial and harmful relationships.

- **Unity and Support (Ecclesiastes 4:12)**

  Solomon provided wisdom beyond measure when he remarked on the strength of a cord of three strands, which symbolizes the power of a couple united with Christ against negative influences. Marital unity, supported by faith, is crucial in overcoming challenges and resisting temptation.

- **Exposing and Addressing Sin (Ephesians 5:11-13)**

Paul speaks to the importance of exposing deeds of darkness. In marriage, this means openly addressing and working through issues like addiction or betrayal rather than allowing them to fester and cause further harm.

- **Christ-Centered Marriage (Colossians 3:12-14)**

    Again, Paul calls us to compassion, kindness, humility, gentleness, and patience, all attributes that should define a Christ-centered marriage. By inviting Christ's influence into their relationship, couples can transform their interactions and build a stronger, more loving union.

Personal Reflection

Think about a time when external influences—perhaps friends, coworkers, or even public figures—shaped your decisions within your marriage. How did these influences affect the unity between you and your spouse? Were your actions and choices aligned with your shared core values, or did they create tension or division? Reflect on how you might better guard your marriage against unhelpful influences, ensuring that your decisions are guided by love, unity, and Christ's example.

_____
_____
_____
_____
_____
_____
_____
_____

Couple's Discussion

Share with one another how external influences have shaped your relationship, both positively and negatively. Confess any ways these influences have caused strain or distraction, and invite God into those areas together. Then, dream about how you can make your marriage a space where Christ's love and guidance are the central forces shaping your decisions, interactions, and shared purpose moving forward.

Day 10: Looking Back

Blessed is the one who perseveres under trial because, having stood the test, that person will receive the crown of life that the Lord has promised to those who love him.

James 1:12

At this point in exploring influence, you are balancing the realities of temptation and the beauty of unity in Christ. James 1:12 reminds us that perseverance through trials brings profound blessings. In marriage, trials test our faith, resilience, and devotion to God and one another, offering a chance to grow stronger together.

Temptation comes in many forms, aiming to distract and destabilize. Yet, each temptation offers a choice—the choice to remain faithful, to prioritize each other, and to follow God's path. In these moments of choosing what is right, your love and commitment are refined.

True unity in Christ is the reward for perseverance. It is not just the absence of conflict but a bond deepened through trials and faith. This unity becomes a powerful reflection of Christ's love within your marriage. Remember, every trial and faithful step moves you closer to the harmony God desires.

📖 Daily Prayer

Lord,

As we navigate the challenges of temptation and strive for unity in our marriage, grant us the strength to persevere. Help us to see the trials we face as opportunities to choose You and each other again and again. Bless our journey with Your wisdom and guide us towards a more profound, meaningful unity in Christ. May our love for each other reflect Your love, and may our marriage be a beacon of hope and faithfulness.

In Jesus' name, Amen.

👫 Fidelity Builder: Mapping Influence

This activity is designed to be a simple yet powerful way to reflect on and appreciate your profound influence on each other's lives, helping to strengthen your bond through greater understanding and intentionality.

Materials Needed

- Sheet of paper
- Two different color pens or colored pencils

Instructions

1. **Individual Reflection**

   Each of you will take a few moments to reflect individually. Think about the ways you influence each other in your daily lives. Consider positive influences (such as encouragement, support, and spiritual guidance) and areas where you might unknowingly have a less positive impact (such as habits or behaviors that may lead to stress or misunderstandings).

   Fold the sheet of paper into thirds. On the left third of the paper, list your spouse at the top, followed by five or six other people, friends, family members, or other influential persons (even those you do not know personally) who have significantly impacted your life below them (top to bottom).

2. **Draw Your Maps**

   On the other two-thirds, you will draw a simple map on separate sheets of paper representing your relationship journey. Use symbols, lines, or words to mark significant moments. These can include milestones (when you met, fell in love, got engaged, etc.), challenges overcome (separations, grief, illness, etc.), moments of deep connection, or even everyday interactions that leave a lasting impression.

   Draw a solid (or black) line from a person to an event they had a positive influence on and a dashed (or red) line from a person to an event they had a negative impact on.

3. **Share and Discuss**

   Take turns sharing your maps with each other. Explain the symbols or moments you have marked, mainly focusing on how your partner's influence helped shape those experiences.

4. **Write It Down**

   After sharing, on the back of your map or on a new sheet of paper, write down one way you have been positively influenced by your partner that you had not fully appreciated before this activity. Also, jot down one new way you would like to influence your partner moving forward, inspired by this reflection and discussion.

5. **Wrap Up**

   Conclude by affirming the positive impacts you have on each other. Commit to being mindful of the influence you wield and to using it to uplift and support one another as you continue your journey together.

As we move forward discussing influence, this map may help you discern some of the negative influences you may need to ask Christ to free from your life.

Harmony In Marriage: Couple's Workbook

Day 11: Bonds of Unity

Therefore, if anyone is in Christ, the new creation has come:[a] *The old has gone, the new is here!*

2 Corinthians 5:17

In the sacred journey of marriage, intertwining your spiritual lives through prayer, worship, and the study of God's Word is beneficial and foundational. As you come together before God, you create a shared space of vulnerability and trust, laying down your individual and collective burdens at His feet. This unity in Christ fortifies your bond, enabling you to face life's storms with a strengthened faith and a more profound love for each other. Remember, your marriage reflects God's love and commitment, a testament to His grace in your lives. Let this divine connection be the cornerstone of your relationship, guiding you to a deeper understanding, respect, and love for one another.

📖 Daily Prayer

Heavenly Father,

We come before You as partners in life and love, seeking to ground our marriage in Your divine wisdom and grace. Help us to prioritize shared prayer and worship, to find guidance and comfort in Your Word, and to seek counsel that aligns with Your will. Guide us to serve together with joy and to immerse ourselves in a Christ-centered community that supports and strengthens our bond. May our marriage be a testament to Your enduring love and faithfulness.

Amen.

📖 Read: Chapter 6, Pages 114-129

Praying and worshiping together is crucial for couples aiming to root their marriage in God's design, creating a deep connection and resilience against life's challenges. Regularly engaging in shared spiritual practices strengthens the marital bond and aligns the couple's path with Christ. Studying God's Word together enlightens and guides the relationship, providing divine wisdom for overcoming obstacles and enhancing mutual understanding. Seeking godly counsel offers external, biblically grounded perspectives that can help navigate marital challenges, promoting growth and unity. Serving together in the community or church fosters a shared mission, deepening the couple's bond and aligning their actions with Christ's teachings. Lastly, fostering a Christ-centered community provides support and accountability, helping couples to grow together in faith and love.

🔑 Key Points

- **Prayer and Worship as Unity (Matthew 18:20)**
  While this verse ultimately concerns Church discipline, it emphasizes Christ's authority in our relationships. Engaging in shared prayer and worship strengthens the marital bond and aligns the couple with God's will, providing a foundation to combat generational sins.

- **Illumination through God's Word (Psalm 119:105)**
  The mutual study of Scripture enlightens couples, offering guidance and clarity, particularly in navigating the shadows cast by generational sins.

- **Value of Godly Counsel (Proverbs 15:22)**
  Seeking wisdom from seasoned believers provides couples with biblical insights to identify and break free from inherited negative patterns.

- **Service as Shared Purpose (1 Peter 4:10)**
  Serving together fosters unity and reflects Christ's love, counteracting the selfish patterns often in generational sins.

- **Community for Growth (Hebrews 10:24-25)**
  A Christ-centered community offers support and accountability, helping couples to grow together and challenge inherited negative behaviors.

✒️ Personal Reflection

Reflect on the negative patterns from your family of origin that you have noticed impacting your relationship. How do these patterns manifest in your interactions with your spouse? Consider how they might influence your communication, conflict resolution, or expectations in your marriage. What steps can you take to address these patterns in a way that fosters growth and healing, both individually and together as a couple? How might inviting God into this process help you break free from these patterns and create a legacy of love, grace, and unity for your marriage?

⟬⟭ Couple's Discussion

Discuss how you can support one another in breaking free from generational sins impacting your lives or marriage. Confess any fears or struggles tied to these patterns and invite God to guide your healing process. Dream together about the Christ-centered legacy you want to build for your family, identifying practical steps to make this vision a reality.

Day 12: Embracing Influence

Submit to one another out of reverence for Christ.

Ephesians 5:21

In today's reflection, let's explore the essence of accepting influence within the sanctity of marriage, an act that extends beyond self to foster a more profound unity in Christ. This mutual acceptance and consideration of our spouse's perspectives are not about eroding our individuality but embracing a collective identity shaped by love and humility. It mirrors the humility of Jesus and teaches us that true strength lies in shared vulnerability and trust, creating a bond where both partners feel profoundly valued and deeply understood.

As we journey together in matrimony, let us aim to cultivate a relationship that reflects Christ's sacrificial love, where mutual respect and submission are not obligations but gifts that enrich our union. May our marriages become beacons of Christ's love, demonstrating the power of godly influence in creating a harmonious and resilient partnership. Let us pray for the wisdom to balance speaking and listening, leading and following, all under Christ's example of love and service.

📖 Daily Prayer

Heavenly Father,

Please guide us to embrace our spouse's influence with open hearts and minds. Help us see each other through Your eyes, valuing our insights and feelings as we build our life together. Teach us to dance harmoniously, reflecting Your love and humility in our marriage.

Amen.

📖 Read: Chapter 7, Pages 130-142

In Chapter 7, "Accepting Influence," the narrative explores the challenges Jake and Ella face in their marriage due to their inability to accept and respect each other's influence genuinely. Their journey reveals that a healthy marriage, rooted in God's design, involves a balance of mutual trust, commitment, and the willingness to embrace each other's perspectives. By understanding that marriage is a covenant of unity and shared purpose, they learn to replace transactional interactions with a deeper, spiritual connection, leading to a more fulfilling partnership grounded in mutual understanding and biblical principles.

🗝 Key Points

- **Mutual Submission in Marriage (Ephesians 5:21)**
  The concept of mutual submission is foundational for a healthy, biblical marriage. It involves both partners valuing and considering each other's opinions and feelings equally. This principle is based on the idea that marriage is a partnership where both individuals should have an equal voice and influence.

- **Covenant vs. Contract (Matthew 9:16)**
  Marriage is described as a sacred covenant, not merely a contract based on conditions and negotiations. This covenant is a commitment made before God, symbolizing a union that goes beyond transactional interactions to mutual trust, respect, and shared life goals.

- **The Importance of Genuine Unity (Ecclesiastes 4:12)**
  True unity in marriage transcends mere agreement and involves a deep, spiritual connection and mutual understanding. It is about moving together in the same direction, guided by shared faith and values, rather than merely compromising or bargaining.

- **Valuing Each Other's Significance (1 Peter 3:7)**
  Recognizing and affirming each other's value and significance within the marriage is crucial. This involves acknowledging and respecting each other's thoughts, feelings, and contributions to the relationship.

- **Spiritual Practice of Accepting Influence (Philippians 2:3-4)**
  Accepting your spouse's influence is a spiritual practice that reflects Christ's humility and love. It requires setting aside ego and selfish desires to prioritize the well-being and perspectives of your partner, fostering a deeper connection and unity.

✒ Personal Reflection

Think back to a recent disagreement with your spouse. Did you take the time to truly listen and consider their perspective, or were you more focused on asserting your viewpoint? Reflect on how your approach affected the outcome of the disagreement and the connection between you both. What steps can you take to ensure that future conflicts are marked by humility, empathy, and a willingness to seek unity rather than being right? How might viewing your spouse's perspective through the lens of Christ's love transform the way you handle disagreements?

⚭ Couple's Discussion

Discuss how you can grow in accepting each other's influence in daily decisions and conflicts. Confess any struggles or hesitations you have faced in valuing your spouse's perspective. Share practical steps you can take together to ensure you both feel heard, respected, and united in your relationship.

Day 13: Being Reconcilable

Get rid of all bitterness, rage and anger, brawling and slander, along with every form of malice. ³² Be kind and compassionate to one another, forgiving each other, just as in Christ God forgave you.

Ephesians 4:31-32

Marriage often brings challenges that test the foundation of your relationship. These moments, though difficult, can either divide or strengthen you. The key to growth lies in repentance and forgiveness. Repentance is more than saying sorry—it is a commitment to change, turning from behaviors that harm your relationship and aligning with God's design for marriage. It requires honesty and humility to confront uncomfortable truths about yourself. Forgiveness, meanwhile, is about releasing resentment and choosing grace. It means letting go of past hurts to embrace healing and reconciliation.

Through repentance and forgiveness, Christ must remain your guide. His love and teachings provide the foundation for a relationship built on trust, unity, and purpose. By leaning on Him, you can overcome discord and move toward a marriage that reflects His grace and love.

📖 Daily Prayer

Heavenly Father,

Guide us through the challenges of marriage with Your wisdom and grace. Help us to genuinely repent for our wrongdoings and to offer forgiveness to our partner, just as You have forgiven us. May our relationship reflect Your love and unity, and may we grow stronger together in Your guidance. Lead us away from past hurts and towards a future filled with Your love and light. In Jesus' name.

Amen.

📖 Read: Chapter 8, Pages 143-154

In this chapter, the fundamental principles revolve around the transformative power of repentance, forgiveness, and the central role of Christ in a marriage. It emphasizes that true repentance involves a profound, heartfelt change, not just superficial apologies, leading to genuine personal growth and relationship healing. Forgiveness is portrayed as a crucial step towards rebuilding trust and moving forward, free from resentment. The narrative underscores that a successful marriage is not merely a partnership between two individuals but a union under Christ's guidance and teachings. This divine influence helps couples navigate past hurts and misunderstandings, fostering a deeper, more meaningful connection. The chapter also highlights the ripple effect of a Christ-centered marriage on families, communities, and beyond, showcasing how such a union can serve as a beacon of hope and a testament to God's love.

Key Points

- **Repentance as Transformation (Acts 3:19)**

    True repentance involves a profound internal change, a turning away from past behaviors and attitudes that have harmed the relationship. It is about seeking God's guidance to better oneself and heal the wounds inflicted on the partnership.

- **Power of Forgiveness (Ephesians 4:32)**

    Forgiveness in marriage is about releasing bitterness and choosing to move forward with love and understanding. It is a mutual journey that heals and strengthens the bond between partners.

- **Christ at the Center (Colossians 3:14)**

    Placing Christ at the center of the marriage transforms it from a mere contractual agreement to a covenantal union bound in Christ's love. This alignment with divine principles guides couples through challenges and enriches their relationship.

- **Impact of a Unified Marriage (Matthew 5:16)**

    A marriage rooted in Christ's teachings extends its influence beyond the couple, impacting families, communities, and strangers. It serves as a living example of God's love and grace.

- **Legacy of Love (Proverbs 13:22)**

    The legacy of a Christ-centered marriage is profound, offering lessons of love, forgiveness, and resilience to future generations and the wider community, thereby perpetuating a cycle of positive influence and spiritual growth.

Personal Reflection

Reflect on a significant experience, such as a past breakup, divorce, job loss, or the death of a loved one, and how it has shaped your reactions and interactions with your spouse. Are there unspoken vows, fears, or attitudes from that experience that you must confess and release to God? Consider how letting go of these burdens could open the door to more incredible healing and unity in your marriage.

___

___

___

___

___

___

ⓒ Couple's Discussion

Discuss how forgiveness plays a role in your relationship. How do you both approach forgiveness after conflicts or misunderstandings? Confess any struggles or barriers that make forgiveness challenging, and share how these moments have affected your connection. Explore ways you can support each other in fostering mutual forgiveness and healing, creating a foundation where love and unity prevail over division.

Day 14: Rooted in Love

Do nothing out of selfish ambition or vain conceit. Rather, in humility value others above yourselves, [4] *not looking to your own interests but each of you to the interests of the others.*

Philippians 2:3-4

As you conclude your journey through understanding the power of influence in your marriage, you must ground your reflections and resolutions in the heart of Christ-like humility. Philippians 2:3-4 does not merely suggest a passive avoidance of selfishness; it actively calls us into a life where our spouse's interests, needs, and well-being take precedence over our desires.

This week, you have explored the multifaceted ways influence weaves through the fabric of your relationship. When rooted in humility and love, influence has the transformative power to build up, encourage, and guide your journey together toward a deeper unity. As you practiced listening, understanding, and supporting each other, you mirrored the humility Christ embodied.

True humility in marriage means recognizing that love is not just about being right or having the last word. It is about valuing your partner's growth, happiness, and spiritual well-being as much as your own. This perspective shift does not diminish your value but elevates the concept of unity as you both grow closer to each other and to God.

As you look forward, let the insights from this week's reflections inspire you to engage in daily acts of love, kindness, and humility. Remember, the most profound influence you can have on your spouse comes through the quiet, consistent demonstration of Christ's love in your actions and words.

📖 Daily Prayer

Heavenly Father,

Thank You for guiding us through this week of growth. Help us root our actions and words in humility and love, valuing our spouse's needs above ours. Teach us to understand, love deeply, and selflessly.

Grant us wisdom to use our influence to strengthen our bond. Let our marriage reflect Your love and unity, pointing others to You as a light in the world.

In Jesus' name, Amen.

🪶 Personal Reflection

Reflect on moments this week when your spouse's influence impacted you, whether positively or negatively. How did these experiences make you feel, and what do they reveal about the depth of your connection? Consider whether your influence in the marriage reflects Christ-like love and humility. Is there an attitude or action you need to confess and change to align more closely with the example of Christ?

_____

_____

_____

_____

_____

_____

_____

💍 Couple's Discussion

Discuss how focusing on Christ's love and humility has shifted the way you influence one another. How has this Christ-centered approach impacted your communication, conflict resolution, or support for each other? Share specific moments from the past week where you saw this influence at work. Reflect on how you can continue nurturing this kind of influence to deepen your connection and strengthen your relationship moving forward.

WEEK THREE: EXPERIENTIAL FIDELITY

Day 15: Experiential Fidelity

Therefore, as God's chosen people, holy and dearly loved, clothe yourselves with compassion, kindness, humility, gentleness and patience. ¹³ Bear with each other and forgive one another if any of you has a grievance against someone. Forgive as the Lord forgave you. ¹⁴ And over all these virtues put on love, which binds them all together in perfect unity.

Colossians 3:12-14

Today, let us reflect on the profound nature of fidelity in our relationships, particularly within the sacred bond of marriage. Fidelity, derived from the Latin word *fidelitatem*, encompasses faithfulness, trustworthiness, and reliability. These are not just terms but the very foundation that strengthens the bond between spouses, reflecting the divine fidelity God shows to us.

In our marriages, fidelity transcends mere physical loyalty; it embodies emotional, mental, and spiritual exclusivity. This commitment fosters an environment where trust, security, and mutual respect can flourish, allowing vulnerability and intimacy to deepen. As we align our actions and choices with God's will, we honor Him and the sanctity of our marriage covenant.

Let us remember that fidelity is a daily choice, a conscious effort to prioritize our spouse's needs and to nurture and protect our relationship. It is about being present, appreciating each other, and growing together in God's grace. As we stand close to our Creator, let us also draw closer to our spouse, embodying the love, respect, and commitment that mirrors God's unwavering faithfulness to us.

📖 Daily Prayer

Heavenly Father,

Thank You for the gift of marriage and the opportunity it presents to reflect Your faithfulness in our lives. Help us to embody the true essence of fidelity in our relationship, not just in words, but in every action and decision we make. Teach us to appreciate our spouse, nurture our bond, and grow together in Your love and grace. May our marriage be a testament to Your divine fidelity, inspiring others and glorifying You. Guide us in maintaining a relationship filled with trust, respect, and mutual growth. In Jesus' name.

Amen.

📖 Read: Part 3 Introduction, Pages 155-158

Marriage fidelity goes beyond being loyal emotionally, mentally, and spiritually. It is the foundation of a secure and intimate bond between spouses, honoring the sacredness of the marital covenant. Infidelity results from deeper issues like abuse, neglect, and unhealthy compromises. To restore marital fidelity, it is essential to address these root problems. Fidelity has six aspects: experiential, intellectual, financial, emotional, sexual, and spiritual. Each contributes to the holistic oneness in marriage, keeping Christ at the center.

🔑 Key Points

- **Comprehensive Nature of Fidelity (1 Corinthians 13:4-7)**

  In a biblical marriage, fidelity encompasses more than just physical loyalty; it involves a deep, spiritual, emotional, and mental commitment to one another, reflecting the comprehensive nature of love described in 1 Corinthians 13:4-7. This holistic approach to fidelity strengthens the bond between spouses, fostering trust, respect, and a profound connection that honors the sanctity of their union.

- **Root Causes of Infidelity**

  Beyond physical betrayal, infidelity can stem from deeper relational fractures such as contempt, emotional neglect, and unresolved conflicts, leading to a breakdown in the marital relationship. These underlying issues, if left unaddressed, can severely impact the spiritual and emotional health of the marriage, highlighting the need for a return to the core biblical values of patience, kindness, and perseverance in love.

- **Dimensions of Marital Fidelity (Ephesians 5:21-33)**

  True marital unity is built on multiple dimensions of fidelity, including intellectual, financial, emotional, sexual, and spiritual. Each aspect contributes to the overall health and sanctity of the marriage, as outlined in Ephesians 5:21-33, which emphasizes mutual submission and respect. Couples can create a resilient, fulfilling, and Christ-centered relationship by actively engaging and nurturing each of these areas.

Harmony In Marriage: Couple's Workbook

✒ Personal Reflection

Reflect on the times you have felt closest to your spouse. What was happening in those moments that made you feel so connected? Were there ways you contributed to that closeness, or are there areas where you could have deepened the connection further? Consider whether your trust and faithfulness reflect Christ's example, and confess any ways you may have fallen short in nurturing that bond.

_____
_____
_____
_____
_____
_____
_____
_____
_____
_____

⚭ Couple's Discussion

Discuss with your spouse the areas within your marriage where you feel there is strong fidelity and areas where it could be improved. Consider how perhaps a history of misplaced hope and a broken or misunderstood concept of influence have contributed to any challenges.

Day 16: A Shared Journey

Two are better than one,
because they have a good return for their labor:
¹⁰ If either of them falls down,
one can help the other up.
But pity anyone who falls
and has no one to help them up.

Ecclesiastes 4:9-10

Life is a tapestry woven from our joys, sorrows, and triumphs. In marriage, this tapestry becomes even richer as two lives blend into one, creating a shared story that is stronger and more beautiful than individual threads. Marriage is not just walking side by side; it is weaving your stories together to build something unique and lasting.

God designed us for companionship, reflecting His relational nature. Ecclesiastes reminds us of the strength of partnership. In marriage, this partnership means lightening each other's burdens, celebrating successes, and growing together through every experience. Each moment, whether challenging or joyful, shapes your relationship and draws you closer to God and each other. Embracing these shared experiences allows your marriage to flourish. Together, you are building a history that reflects God's love and strengthens the bond that holds you through life's ups and downs.

Daily Prayer

Heavenly Father,

Thank You for the gift of companionship and the blessing of marriage. Help us cherish and learn from every experience we share. Teach us to support one another, lift each other up, and celebrate our victories together. May our shared journey deepen our love, strengthen our bond, and draw us closer to You. Guide us in creating a shared narrative that honors You and reflects Your love and faithfulness. In Jesus' name.

Amen.

📖 Read: Chapter 9, Pages 159-168

This section of Chapter 9 introduces the idea of "Experiential Fidelity" within marriage, emphasizing the importance of shared experiences in shaping the personalities of individuals and the journey of a couple together. It discusses how both positive and negative experiences can affect beliefs, behaviors, and the overall dynamics of a relationship. The chapter highlights the value of facing challenges as a team, fostering spiritual growth, and creating a shared story that strengthens the bond between spouses. It also warns against the subtle forms of experiential infidelity where couples grow apart by neglecting shared activities and moments, leading to emotional and spiritual disconnection. The text underlines the necessity of actively seeking out shared experiences that align with God's design, thereby enriching the marriage and honoring the divine covenant.

🔑 Key Points

- **Shared Growth through Challenges (James 1:2-4)**

    Experiences, especially challenging ones, refine and strengthen a couple's faith and relationship. Facing trials together fosters unity and a deeper understanding of each other, aligning the couple's path closer to Christ.

- **Creating a Shared Narrative (Ecclesiastes 4:9-12)**

    Building a life together filled with shared experiences and memories strengthens the marital bond and reflects the unity God intends for marriage. This shared narrative is foundational to a strong, enduring relationship.

- **The Importance of Spiritual Connection (1 John 1:3)**

    Engaging in spiritual activities together, such as prayer and worship, deepens the couple's connection with each other and with God, fostering experiential fidelity (Matthew 18:20).

- **The Danger of Neglect (Hebrews 10:24-25)**

    Neglecting shared rituals and experiences can lead to experiential infidelity, eroding the foundation of the marriage. Couples must prioritize and cherish their time together to maintain a strong bond.

- **Healing and Growth from Past Experiences (Isaiah 43:18-19)**

    Understanding and empathizing with each other's past experiences can lead to healing and growth within the marriage, allowing for surrender, forgiveness, and most importantly grace. Open communication about past pains and joys helps build a resilient and empathetic relationship.

🪶 Personal Reflection

Reflect on a shared experience with your spouse, whether positive or challenging, that brought you closer together. What aspects of that experience made it so meaningful or transformative? Are there ways you can confess missed opportunities to create such moments? Consider how you can intentionally cultivate more experiences that strengthen your connection and honor the commitment you share.

_____
_____
_____
_____
_____
_____
_____
_____
_____
_____

💍 Couple's Discussion

Reflect on a challenging experience you faced together as a couple. How did it impact your relationship, and what did you learn about each other and God through it? Share how this experience has shaped your understanding of your marriage and discuss how you can use these insights to navigate future challenges and grow closer as a couple.

Day 17: Growing Together

Carry each other's burdens, and in this way you will fulfill the law of Christ.

Galatians 6:2

Today, we reflect on the journey of marriage, a path filled with shared experiences that shape and define our union. Marriage, as depicted through the story of Leah and Samuel, begins with excitement and passion, a testament to God's design for companionship and love. However, as time progresses, the initial spark can fade, replaced by routine and individual pursuits, leading to what can be termed 'experiential infidelity'—a gradual drifting apart not just physically but in shared dreams and adventures.

Yet, the Bible reminds us that two are better than one. This principle is about physical presence and sharing life's burdens, joys, and spiritual walk. In marriage, we are called to support each other, to lift each other up, and to face life's challenges together, reflecting God's faithfulness and love.

As we navigate through different phases of marriage—from the honeymoon period to facing external challenges, from the joys of family and parenthood to rediscovering our bond and aging together—each stage offers unique opportunities for growth, deeper connection, and spiritual enrichment. These experiences, whether joyous or challenging, are not meant to be walked alone but together, hand in hand, with God at the center of our union.

📖 Daily Prayer

Heavenly Father,

Thank You for the gift of marriage and the journey it entails. Help us to cherish and nurture the bond we share with our spouse. Teach us to embrace each moment, whether filled with joy or challenges, as an opportunity to grow closer to each other and to You. Grant us the wisdom to navigate the transitions of life with grace, understanding, and mutual respect. Remind us to support each other, to lift each other up, and to face life's challenges together under Your guidance. May our marriage be a testament to Your enduring love and faithfulness. In Jesus' name.

Amen.

📖 Read: Chapter 9, Pages 168-175

The text describes the experiential journey of a couple, Leah and Samuel, from their initial meeting through various phases of their marriage. It highlights the importance of shared experiences in deepening their bond and navigating life's challenges together. Initially, their relationship flourished with shared activities and spiritual growth. Still, as life's routine set in, they found themselves drifting apart due to a lack of shared experiences, leading to what is termed as 'experiential infidelity.' The narrative then explores the universal stages of marriage: the honeymoon phase, facing external challenges, joys of family and parenthood, rediscovering the bond after children leave home, and aging together. Each phase presents unique challenges and opportunities for growth, emphasizing the need for intentional effort, communication, and reliance on God to maintain a robust and fulfilling marriage.

🗝 Key Points

- **Foundational Experiences (Genesis 2:24)**

  The early stages of a relationship set the tone for marital unity. As couples navigate the honeymoon phase, they must integrate their individual backgrounds and expectations into a cohesive life plan. This period is crucial for establishing mutual respect, communication, and shared norms, reflecting the biblical principle of leaving and cleaving to create one flesh.

- **Navigating Life's Challenges Together (Galatians 6:2)**

  External pressures such as financial difficulties, health crises, and work-related stress can strain a marriage. However, these challenges allow couples to demonstrate resilience, support each other, and deepen their reliance on God, mirroring the call to bear one another's burdens.

- **The Joys and Trials of Parenthood (Ephesians 6:4)**

  The arrival of children marks a significant shift in a couple's life, introducing new responsibilities and joys. Balancing parenting with maintaining a strong marital bond is essential, aligning with the scriptural emphasis on the family unit and the parental role in nurturing and instruction.

- **Rediscovering Each Other (Romans 12:2)**

  The "empty nest" phase allows couples to renew their focus on each other and explore new shared interests. This period is an opportunity to strengthen their marital and spiritual connection, reminiscent of the biblical call to continually renew and transform our lives.

- **Aging Gracefully Together (Proverbs 31:10-31)**

In their later years, couples face the realities of aging and health challenges and reflect on their legacy. This phase encourages deep introspection, mutual support, and a celebration of shared life, echoing the biblical perspective on the value of wisdom, experience, and enduring love.

🪶 Personal Reflection

Reflect on the phase of marriage you are currently in. What blessings have you experienced, and what challenges have emerged? Are there areas where you may need to confess struggles or missed opportunities to grow together? Consider how you can embrace this phase with gratitude and seek God's guidance to navigate its unique joys and difficulties.

_____
_____
_____
_____
_____
_____
_____
_____
_____
_____
_____

💍 Couple's Discussion

Talk with your spouse about ways to create more meaningful shared experiences that strengthen your bond in this phase of your marriage. Share any fears or obstacles hindering this and invite God into the conversation. Discuss practical ways to ensure He remains at the center of these moments, deepening your connection both with each other and with Him.

Day 18: Delight Together

Take delight in the Lord,
and he will give you the desires of your heart.

Psalm 37:4

In the heart of every couple lies a treasure trove of desires and dreams. These are not just individual aspirations but shared visions that bloom from the soil of togetherness. Today's verse, Psalm 37:4, invites us to find our deepest joy and satisfaction in the Lord. It is a gentle reminder that when we align our lives, including our relationships, with God, He lovingly attends to the desires of our hearts.

In the context of marriage, this verse beckons couples to root their relationship in the joy found in God. It is about seeing each other through God's lens, appreciating the partner He has provided, and finding new ways to celebrate this divine gift. Delighting in the Lord together paves the way for a deeper, more joyful connection.

Consider this: when both partners seek joy in God, their shared experiences become richer and more meaningful. Activities like the Date Night Planner are not just about having fun or breaking the routine; they are opportunities to explore and express the joy found in God's presence. They become acts of worship, avenues through which you both can experience and celebrate God's goodness and creativity.

Today, let us focus on finding delight in the Lord within the context of your marriage. Let your shared activities, plans, and dreams express this more profound joy. As you delight yourselves in the Lord, watch how He beautifully orchestrates the desires of your hearts into a harmonious melody that resonates with His love.

📖 Daily Prayer

Heavenly Father,

We come to You as partners in life, seeking to find our most profound joy in Your presence. Teach us to delight ourselves in You above all else. As we explore new experiences and create memories, let our hearts remain anchored in Your love. Bless our plans and dreams, and mold them according to Your will. May our relationship be a testament to the joy and fulfillment of living for You.

In Jesus' name, we pray, Amen.

👫 Fidelity Builder: Date Planner

This activity is more than just organizing fun outings; it is about prioritizing your relationship and creating shared experiences that deepen your connection. Enjoy the spontaneity, cherish the moments, and let each date strengthen the beautiful harmony of your partnership.

Materials Needed

- A jar or any container you both love
- Strips of paper or popsicle sticks
- A pen or marker
- A notebook or planner

Instructions

1. **Brainstorm Date Ideas**

    Sit down together and brainstorm a variety of date ideas. These can range from simple at-home activities to more adventurous outings. Think about experiences you have always wanted to try, local places you would love to visit, or hobbies you would enjoy exploring together. Aim for a good mix of indoor and outdoor activities, considering different seasons and interests.

2. **Write Them Down**

    Once you have a list, take turns writing each date idea on a strip of paper or popsicle stick. Feel free to decorate or color-code the strips based on categories (e.g., outdoor, indoor, free, requires planning, etc.).

3. **Fill Your Date Jar**

    Place all your date ideas into the jar. Shake it up to mix the suggestions thoroughly, adding the element of surprise for when you draw your next date night adventure.

4. **Create Your Date Night Planner**

    Use the notebook or planner to schedule regular date nights. Decide together how often is practical for you to have a date night—weekly, bi-weekly, or monthly. On each scheduled date night, take turns drawing an idea from the jar. Whatever you pick is your plan for that evening!

5. **Plan and Enjoy**

    Once you have drawn your date night activity, spend a moment planning any necessary details. Do you need to make reservations? Buy tickets? Or simply set the scene at home? Then, dive into the experience together, making the most of your time.

Bonus Tips

- After completing a date, write a short note about what you did and what you enjoyed about it in your planner. This becomes a keepsake of your shared experiences.
- Feel free to continuously add new date ideas to the jar as you think of them or discover new interests together.
- You do not need to agree on every date night, part of this is learning more about your spouse. So, add things to the mix that you would love to introduce to your spouse (for example, maybe your husband really needs a pedicure).

Day 19: Silent Drift

Has not the one God made you? You belong to him in body and spirit. And what does the one God seek? Godly offspring.[a] So be on your guard, and do not be unfaithful to the wife of your youth.

Malachi 2:15

Marriage is a sacred bond that connects two souls spiritually and emotionally, not just physically. Although fictional, Leah and Samuel's story is relatable to many couples. It is a gradual disconnection over time, rather than sudden events, affecting the shared moments and experiences. God designed marriage as a partnership where two people can share their lives, dreams, and challenges. Together, they form a stronger bond than they could alone, like strands of a rope. This divine design is meant to reflect the unity and love found in Christ - patient, kind, and enduring.

However, they will drift apart if couples stop sharing their lives, daily moments, dreams, and challenges. This distance is physical, emotional, and spiritual, as warned in the Bible. Unity is strength, while isolation can be dangerous. Today's devotional is a reminder to reflect on the shared journey of your marriage. Are you and your partner growing closer, or are you drifting apart? Remember, the small moments, the daily decision to turn towards each other, build a lifetime of love and companionship.

📖 Daily Prayer

Heavenly Father,

Guide us to cherish and nurture our marital bond with the same love, patience, and commitment You show us. Please help us recognize and address any neglect or distance in our relationship. Strengthen our communication, deepen our shared experiences, and rekindle our spiritual unity. May our marriage reflect Your love and grace, growing stronger and more intimate each day.

Amen.

📖 Read: Chapter 9, Pages 175-184

This text explores the gradual emotional and experiential distancing between Leah and Samuel, highlighting the subtle decline in their shared experiences and interactions. Initially bonded by deep love and shared activities, their relationship begins to suffer as they engage less with each other and more with individual pursuits, leading to coexistence rather than partnership. This distancing, termed experiential infidelity, lacks dramatic confrontations but significantly impacts the marriage's intimacy and spiritual unity.

🔑 Key Points

- **Gradual Distancing in Relationships (1 Peter 1:22)**
  Like the slow accumulation of grains in an hourglass, small instances of neglect can lead to significant emotional distance. Biblical teachings emphasize the importance of vigilance and continuous nurturing in relationships, reflecting the principle that love must be actively maintained, as suggested by the call to love one another deeply from the heart.

- **The Importance of Shared Experiences (Proverbs 27:17)**
  Shared experiences are foundational to building and maintaining married couples' bonds. The Bible highlights the strength of unity and shared endeavors, underscoring the importance of companionship and mutual support in overcoming life's challenges.

- **Communication and Intentionality (Ephesians 4:15, 25)**
  Effective communication and intentional engagement are crucial in preventing and addressing experiential infidelity. Scriptures advocate for open, honest communication and mutual understanding, reflecting the teachings on speaking the truth in love and fostering peace and unity.

- **Impact of Neglect on Intimacy (1 Timothy 5:8)**
  The decline in emotional and spiritual intimacy due to experiential infidelity mirrors the biblical warnings against neglect and complacency in relationships. The call to not neglect one's family can be extended to the emotional and spiritual neglect that harms marital intimacy.

- **Spiritual Disconnection (Romans 6:20-23)**
  A shared spiritual journey is central to a Christian marriage. Experiential infidelity can weaken this spiritual bond, contrary to the biblical model of a marriage that reflects Christ's relationship with the Church. This ultimately leads to temptation and sin. Maintaining spiritual intimacy through prayer, worship, and shared faith experiences is crucial for upholding the marital covenant.

✒ Personal Reflection

Reflect on how you seek connection in your marriage. Have there been times when you reached out for your spouse's attention or companionship, and they did not respond as you hoped? How did this make you feel, and how did you react? Consider whether your spouse fully understood your desire for connection. Are there ways you can confess any frustration or hurt while also showing them grace? How might you be more vulnerable and transparent about your needs, creating opportunities for deeper intimacy and understanding?

_____
_____
_____
_____
_____
_____
_____
_____
_____
_____

💍 Couple's Discussion

Share with your spouse moments when you felt especially connected or disconnected in your relationship. Be honest about what actions or circumstances contributed to those feelings. Confess any personal struggles that may have created distance, and discuss how you can intentionally cultivate more moments of connection while addressing the causes of disconnection together.

Harmony In Marriage: Couple's Workbook

Day 20: Renewing Connection

I can do all this through him who gives me strength.

Philippians 4:13

Marriage is a journey that requires effort and dedication, bringing together two unique individuals. While love is its foundation, a lasting marriage needs more—this is where Christ comes in. He provides strength, wisdom, and guidance to navigate challenges and nurture a bond grounded in His love. Christ is an active participant in your marriage, offering qualities like patience, forgiveness, humility, and selflessness.

Making Christ the cornerstone means seeking His will in decisions, turning to Scripture for wisdom, and praying together. It also involves stepping out of your comfort zone as a couple—whether by trying new things, serving others, or improving communication. A marriage centered on Christ thrives, reflecting His love through patience, kindness, and endurance. With His help, you can face challenges together, building a strong, resilient relationship filled with peace and joy.

📖 Daily Prayer

Lord Jesus,

We come before You today, grateful for Your unending love and strength. In our journey of marriage, remind us that it is through You alone that we can truly grow and thrive as a couple. Help us to lean on You in times of distance and difficulty and to find joy and purpose in our shared journey. Guide us in rediscovering the love and passion that brought us together, and inspire us to live intentionally and passionately with You at the center of our relationship. Strengthen our bond, Lord, and help us reflect Your love in all we do. In Your holy name, we pray.

Amen.

📖 Read: Chapter 5, Pages 184-195

Samuel and Leah's marriage faced challenges due to a lack of shared experiences and communication, leading to a growing distance between them. Samuel's mentor, David, advised him on the importance of intentional time together, revisiting shared hobbies, and the power of prayer and open communication to reconnect. He suggested new shared experiences and celebrating milestones to strengthen their bond. The narrative emphasizes the importance of experiential fidelity in marriage, highlighting that shared experiences, challenges, and spiritual practices can deepen the couple's connection and lead to a more fulfilling union. The story concludes with Samuel and Leah taking steps to rekindle their relationship, illustrating the transformative power of intentional, shared experiences in marriage.

🗝 Key Points

- **Intentional Time Together (Genesis 2:2-3)**

  Just as God set aside the Sabbath for rest and connection, couples should carve out dedicated time for each other to foster intimacy and understanding.

- **Shared Spiritual Practices (1 Peter 3:7)**

  Like how Jesus prayed with His disciples, emphasizing unity and faith, husbands should lead their wives, and families to engage in joint spiritual activities like prayer and Bible study to strengthen their bond and align with God's will.

- **Open Communication (Ephesians 4:15)**

  Following Paul's advice to speak the truth in love, couples are encouraged to express their feelings and concerns openly to maintain a healthy and transparent relationship.

- **Celebrating Milestones and Creating New Experiences (Joshua 4:6-7)**

  Echoing the biblical principle of remembering and celebrating God's faithfulness, couples should commemorate their shared history and seek new adventures to enrich their relationship.

- **Experiential Fidelity and Shared Growth (Hebrews 10:24-25)**

  By consistently participating in shared experiences, especially those rooted in faith like worship and community service, couples can strengthen their connection and encourage each other toward love and good deeds.

✒ Personal Reflection

Reflect on the balance between your pursuits and the activities you share with your spouse. Are there areas where you could intentionally invest more time and energy into experiences that strengthen your connection and help you grow together? Are there hobbies or commitments hindering your relationship and need to be reconsidered or eliminated? Confess how your choices might have prioritized personal interests over your marriage, and consider how you can refocus on building unity and joy together.

💍 Couple's Discussion

Talk with your spouse about experiential fidelity and how it plays a role in your relationship. Share any feelings of distance or neglect in your shared experiences and confess any personal barriers that may have contributed. Identify activities or interests you have set aside and discuss how you can intentionally reintegrate them to strengthen your emotional and spiritual bond.

Day 21: Everyday Joy

Enjoy life with your wife, whom you love, all the days of this meaningless life that God has given you under the sun—all your meaningless days. For this is your lot in life and in your toilsome labor under the sun.

Ecclesiastes 9:9

As we wrap up our reflection on experiential fidelity, Ecclesiastes reminds us to treasure each moment with our spouse. This Scripture is not about despair but an invitation to find joy in the everyday experiences shared with the one you love. It is not about grand gestures but about seeing God's presence in the ordinary—in shared laughter, quiet evenings, and even in challenges.

Experiential fidelity means being fully present and valuing your time together as a gift from God. You may have discovered new ways to connect and build meaningful memories this week. Remember, it is the quality of your interactions that strengthens your bond. Focus on your spouse intentionally, celebrating the small joys and offering unwavering support through life's ups and downs.

📖 Daily Prayer

Lord,

Thank You for the gift of companionship and the joy found in the journey with my spouse. Please help us to see the beauty in our shared experiences, no matter how small or mundane they may seem. Teach us to cherish each other and to recognize Your presence in every moment of our lives together. Guide us in maintaining a solid bond of experiential fidelity anchored in Your love and grace.

Amen.

🪶 Personal Reflection

Reflect on an activity or routine that you usually do on your own. How might you invite your spouse to join you in this activity to build greater connection and experiential fidelity? Are there adjustments you could make to ensure it becomes a shared, enjoyable experience for both of you? Confess any reluctance you may feel about making this change and consider how prioritizing togetherness in these moments could strengthen your bond.

_____
_____
_____
_____
_____
_____
_____
_____
_____
_____

⚭ Couple's Discussion

Talk with your spouse about changes or new practices you want to implement daily, weekly, monthly, and yearly to strengthen experiential fidelity. Confess any past struggles in prioritizing shared experiences and reflect on what has kept you from being more intentional. Discuss how to make these practices a natural part of your relationship, reinforcing your bond and deepening your connection. Create a concrete plan together to move forward with purpose.

WEEK FOUR: INTELLECTUAL FIDELITY

Day 22: Intellectual Fidelity

Be completely humble and gentle; be patient, bearing with one another in love. ³ Make every effort to keep the unity of the Spirit through the bond of peace.

Ephesians 4:2-3

Reflecting on your marriage, remember the strength and unity that Christ provides. A biblical marriage thrives on intellectual fidelity—a shared commitment to understanding and supporting each other's growth. Genuine connection and renewal, however, come through Christ.

Consider how you can lean on Christ to bridge intellectual gaps, whether by studying the Bible, praying, or attending church together. Embrace growth opportunities as individuals and as a couple, trusting that through Christ, all things are possible.

Let Christ's love and wisdom guide every decision, big or small. With Him as your foundation, you can face challenges with faith and hope, building a deeper and more fulfilling marriage together.

Daily Prayer

Lord,

Guide us to honor and respect each other's thoughts and beliefs within our marriage. Please help us to foster an environment of open communication and mutual understanding. Strengthen our bond through shared spiritual practices and a deep commitment to Your word. Remind us to value each other's intellectual contributions and to guard against any form of intellectual infidelity. May our marriage reflect Your wisdom, love, and unity.

Amen.

Read: Chapter 10, Pages 196-201

In a biblical marriage, intellectual fidelity encompasses honoring and respecting each other's thoughts, ideas, and perspectives, fostering an environment of openness and constructive dialogue. This form of fidelity strengthens the marital bond by encouraging deep engagement with each other's beliefs and aspirations, thereby enriching the couple's understanding and honoring God in body, spirit, and mind. Intellectual validation, rooted in mutual respect and appreciation, bolsters resilience, fosters optimism, and deepens relational bonds, enhancing the quality and harmony of relationships. Furthermore, intellectual worth is closely linked to spiritual well-being, influencing one's connection with God and understanding of their divine purpose. Recognizing and nurturing intellectual value within a marriage is crucial for personal growth, spiritual connection, and the fulfillment of God's design for a harmonious partnership.

🗝 Key Points

- **Mutual Respect and Understanding (Proverbs 27:17)**

    Intellectual fidelity in marriage involves mutual respect and understanding of each other's thoughts and beliefs. This aligns with biblical teachings emphasizing the importance of wisdom, experience, and the respectful exchange of ideas. In a spiritually aligned marriage, both partners are encouraged to grow in knowledge and support each other's intellectual pursuits, reflecting the biblical principle of iron sharpening iron.

- **Open Communication (Ephesians 4:25)**

    The Bible emphasizes the importance of honest and loving communication. In a marriage, this means creating a safe space for each partner to express their thoughts and feelings without fear of dismissal or ridicule. Open communication fosters intellectual intimacy, allowing both partners to share their insights, doubts, and aspirations, strengthening their bond and mutual understanding.

- **Shared Spiritual Practices (Romans 12:10)**

    Engaging in shared spiritual practices, such as prayer and Bible study, is a form of intellectual fidelity that deepens the couple's connection with each other and with God. These practices allow couples to explore their faith together, challenge each other's understanding, and grow spiritually, reinforcing the biblical model of a marriage that honors God.

- **Valuing Each Other's Contributions (1 Corinthians 12:7)**

    Recognizing and valuing each other's intellectual contributions reinforces a sense of worth and belonging within the marriage. The Bible speaks to the value of everyone's unique gifts and perspectives. In marriage, acknowledging and appreciating these contributions fosters a supportive environment where both partners can thrive intellectually and spiritually.

- **Guarding Against Intellectual Infidelity (James 3:17)**

    Intellectual infidelity, characterized by neglecting or devaluing a partner's thoughts and ideas, can erode the foundation of trust and respect in a marriage. The Bible warns against behaviors that lead to disunity and discord. Couples are encouraged to remain vigilant against such tendencies, striving instead for a relationship that reflects mutual respect, understanding, and a shared commitment to God's wisdom.

🪶 Personal Reflection

Reflect on how you engage with your spouse's thoughts and ideas. Are there times when you may have unintentionally dismissed or undervalued their contributions? Think of specific moments when this might have happened and how it impacted your connection. Confess any tendencies to overlook their input and consider how you can respond more intentionally to honor and encourage their perspective, fostering a deeper and more intellectually fulfilling relationship.

_____
_____
_____
_____
_____
_____
_____
_____
_____
_____
_____
_____

💍 Couple's Discussion

Share with your spouse how you perceive and value each other's intellectual contributions to your relationship. Confess any moments where you may have dismissed or undervalued their thoughts and ideas, and express how it made you feel when your own ideas were overlooked. Identify ways to enhance intellectual fidelity, such as setting aside time for deep conversations, exploring shared interests, or engaging in activities that challenge and grow your minds together. Commit to a plan that fosters mutual respect and connection in this area.

Harmony In Marriage: Couple's Workbook

Day 23: Opening a Channel

My dear brothers and sisters, take note of this: Everyone should be quick to listen, slow to speak and slow to become angry…

James 1:19

Intellectual intimacy is just as important in marriage as emotional and physical connections. When partners dismiss, interrupt, or undervalue each other's input, it can lead to feelings of isolation and a lack of respect. God designed marriage as a union of hearts and minds, where mutual growth and encouragement play a vital role. Proverbs 27:17 reminds us, "As iron sharpens iron, so one person sharpens another."

A thriving marriage values and engages with each partner's thoughts and ideas, fostering respect and connection. Strengthening intellectual intimacy requires honesty, humility, and active listening. Reflect on your interactions—are there ways you can better support and value your spouse's ideas? Marriage is a journey of continual growth, grounded in respect and love.

📖 Daily Prayer

Heavenly Father,

Thank You for the gift of marriage and the joy of sharing life together. Help us value intellectual intimacy by listening actively, respecting each other's ideas, and having meaningful conversations. Forgive moments of dismissiveness or belittlement and guide us to grow in understanding and respect. Bless our marriage with Your grace, and may it reflect Your love and bring strength and joy to our lives.

In Jesus' name, Amen.

📖 Read: Chapter 10, Pages 201-207

Intellectual fidelity in marriage is grounded in respecting and valuing each other's thoughts and ideas, which is crucial for a healthy and enriching relationship. It involves active listening, considering each other's input seriously, and maintaining open communication to prevent feelings of dismissiveness or isolation. Intellectual fidelity strengthens the bond between partners by fostering an environment of mutual respect and understanding, allowing both individuals to grow and navigate life's challenges together. Recognizing and addressing behaviors that undermine this intellectual bond, such as dismissiveness, interrupting, and belittling, is essential for maintaining a strong and supportive marital relationship.

🔑 Key Points

- **Recognizing and Addressing Dismissiveness (Ephesians 4:29)**
  Dismissiveness in a relationship can undermine a partner's confidence and self-worth. It is crucial to acknowledge and validate each other's ideas and passions to foster a supportive environment.

- **Valuing Partner's Input (Philippians 2:3-4)**
  Intellectual fidelity involves valuing and considering your partner's suggestions and contributions as significant. Ignoring or undervaluing these can lead to resentment and detachment.

- **Open and Honest Communication (James 1:19)**
  Maintaining open lines of communication is essential for intellectual intimacy. Couples should avoid secrets and make decisions together, reflecting mutual respect and unity.

- **Mutual Respect and Understanding (1 Peter 3:7)**
  Belittling or mocking a partner's ideas can cause harm and create a barrier to intellectual intimacy. Respectful dialogue and understanding are foundational to a healthy relationship.

- **Shared Spiritual and Intellectual Growth (Ecclesiastes 4:9-12)**
  Encouraging each other's intellectual and spiritual growth strengthens the marital bond and aligns the couple more closely with God's purpose for their union.

🖋 Personal Reflection

Reflect on times when you may have been dismissive or not fully present during conversations with your spouse. How might your behavior have impacted the conversation and your spouse's willingness to share or be vulnerable in these moments? Confess any patterns of inattentiveness or dismissiveness, and consider practical ways to improve your listening skills. How can you show genuine interest and value in your spouse's thoughts and ideas, fostering deeper connection and trust?

_____

_____

⚭ Couple's Discussion

Share moments when you felt intellectually neglected or belittled in your relationship. Confess how you may have dismissed or undervalued your spouse's thoughts, and express how it has impacted your connection. Discuss how you can create a more supportive and engaging environment that fosters intellectual growth and respect. Set specific goals for improving communication through dedicated discussion time, shared learning activities, or seeking outside support when needed.

Day 24: Navigating the Storm

God is our refuge and strength,
an ever-present help in trouble.
² Therefore we will not fear, though the earth give way
and the mountains fall into the heart of the sea,
³ though its waters roar and foam
and the mountains quake with their surging.

Psalm 46:1-3

In marriage, crises serve as profound tests, challenging the unity and strength of our bonds. These moments demand more than love; they require intellectual fidelity – a deep commitment to respect, understand, and support each other's thoughts and aspirations. In these turbulent times, the true depth of a partnership is revealed. Intellectual fidelity is not merely about agreement but about fostering an environment where both individuals feel heard, valued, and supported.

When faced with adversity, the instinct may be to withdraw or invalidate each other's feelings, but this only leads to further isolation and hurt. Instead, we are called to lean into the storm together, engaging in honest, empathetic communication. It is about acknowledging each other's perspectives, fears, and dreams and working collaboratively towards solutions. This approach navigates the immediate crisis and strengthens the relationship for future challenges.

📖 Daily Prayer

Heavenly Father,

During life's storms, guide us to anchor our relationship in You. Help us to practice intellectual fidelity, respecting and valuing each other's thoughts, ideas, and dreams. Grant us the wisdom to listen deeply, communicate openly, and support each other unconditionally. In times of disagreement or misunderstanding, remind us of the love that brought us together and the shared journey we are on.

Strengthen our bond, Lord, so that we may face challenges as a united front, drawing on each other's strengths and Your divine guidance. Help us to remember that together, with You at our center, we can overcome any obstacle. Teach us to grow from every experience, turning trials into testimonies of Your faithfulness and love.

In Jesus' name, we pray,

Amen.

📖 Read: Chapter 10, Pages 207-212

In "Crisis Mode," the narrative explores the challenges faced by Lucas and Kiera, highlighting the importance of intellectual fidelity in marriage, especially during times of crisis. Lucas's dream of starting a business is dismissed by Kiera, leading to his silent withdrawal and a growing distance between them. This situation worsens with Kiera's mother's illness, placing additional strain on their relationship and Lucas's personal aspirations. The story underscores the detrimental effects of intellectual infidelity, such as dismissiveness, belittling, and isolation. It contrasts these with the strength and unity fostered through mutual respect, open communication, and shared problem-solving in a marriage.

🔑 Key Points

- **Intellectual Fidelity in Crisis (Proverbs 15:22)**
  Intellectual fidelity involves respecting and valuing each other's ideas and contributions, which is especially crucial during crises. Partners can navigate challenges more effectively When they actively engage and support each other's intellectual input.

- **Consequences of Dismissiveness (Proverbs 18:13-14)**
  Dismissing a partner's ideas or dreams, as seen with Lucas's business plan, can lead to silent compromises, where one partner withdraws to avoid conflict. This leads to a lack of genuine communication and shared problem-solving.

- **Impact of Silent Compromises (Ephesians 4:25)**
  Silent compromises, where spouses avoid engaging, communicating, or confronting due to intellectual infidelity, can lead to resentment, misunderstanding, and emotional distance, weakening the marital bond and making it harder to face life's challenges as a united front.

- **Navigating Crises Together (John 17:21-23)**

    Effective crisis management requires open dialogue, mutual respect, and valuing each partner's perspective. This collaborative approach strengthens the relationship and fosters a deeper understanding and connection between partners. We are called to mirror the Jesus's unity with the Father and the Spirit.

- **Overcoming Intellectual Infidelity (Colossians 3:9-10)**

    Recognizing and addressing behaviors that contribute to intellectual infidelity, such as belittling or gaslighting, are crucial for restoring trust and respect in the relationship, enabling couples to face challenges together with combined strength and wisdom.

Personal Reflection

Reflect on a time when you faced a significant decision during a stressful period. Did you seek and genuinely value your spouse's input, or did you decide on your own? Consider how your approach affected your relationship and communication. Confess any tendencies to act unilaterally and think about how involving your spouse more intentionally could strengthen your partnership and trust in the future.

_____
_____
_____
_____
_____
_____
_____
_____
_____

Couple's Discussion

Reflect on a recent crisis or major decision you faced as a couple. How did each of you contribute to the conversation and decision-making process? Confess moments when you may have dismissed or disregarded your spouse's input, and acknowledge times when you felt unheard. Discuss whether intellectual fidelity was upheld or challenged and explore ways to strengthen mutual respect and understanding in future challenges.

Day 25: Learning Together

Let the message of Christ dwell among you richly as you teach and admonish one another with all wisdom through psalms, hymns, and songs from the Spirit, singing to God with gratitude in your hearts.

Colossians 3:16

In marriage, the shared pursuit of wisdom and growth strengthens the connection between partners, fostering a deeper and more meaningful relationship. Colossians 3:16 encourages us to root our relationships in Christ's teachings, embracing intellectual curiosity and spiritual depth.

Marriage thrives when both partners contribute their unique perspectives. This diversity enriches the relationship, creating a bond built on respect, understanding, and the desire to see the world through each other's eyes. By engaging with scripture, exploring new ideas, and growing together, couples can build a connection that goes beyond the surface.

This journey is not about uniformity but celebrating each other's differences and learning from them. By creating an environment of learning and encouragement anchored in Christ's love, marriage becomes a dynamic partnership. Together, you grow spiritually and intellectually, reflecting God's design for unity and diversity.

Daily Prayer

Dear Lord,

We pray for the wisdom to nurture our intellectual bond, guided by Your word and love. Please help us cherish and learn from our differences, grow in understanding, and deepen our connection with every shared experience. May our conversations and explorations glorify You and strengthen the harmony of our marriage.

In Jesus' name, we pray, Amen.

Fidelity Builder: Teach Me Something New

The objective of this activity is designed to deepen your intellectual and experiential bond by exploring new territories of knowledge and skill, emphasizing the joy of learning and growth as a couple.

Materials Needed

- A jar or container

- Pieces of paper
- Pens

Instructions

1. **Create Your Idea Jar**

   Each of you separately take some time to write down various interests, hobbies, topics, or activities that intrigue you (but you are not familiar with) on separate pieces of paper. These can range from culinary skills, massage techniques, historical mysteries, to language basics to crafting methods, or even Bible knowledge, anything goes so long as its new. Feel free to include anything that sparks curiosity, regardless of whether it is a shared interest or something entirely new to one or both of you.

2. **Fill the Jar**

   Place all the written ideas into your jar. Mix them up so your choices will be a surprise.

3. **Pick and Research**

   Starting today, each partner draws a paper from the jar, revealing their challenge for the week. You then have a set amount of time, take an hour or so to research the subject. If it is an activity (like a new cuisine or a special massage), prepare to perform it. If it is a topic of knowledge (like a historical event or a scientific principle), prepare a fun and engaging way to teach it to your partner.

4. **Share and Learn**

   Set aside a special time this evening to take turns sharing what you have learned or demonstrate the new skill. If it is a cuisine, perhaps prepare a meal together based on the new recipe you have researched. If it is a massage technique, take turns giving each other a relaxing treatment. For topics of knowledge, make your presentation interactive and engaging - think of it as storytelling or a mini-classroom session where curiosity leads the way.

5. **Reflect and Discuss**

   After each teaching session, take some time to discuss what you have learned. Did the activity or knowledge challenge your perspectives? Did it spark a newfound interest for one or both of you? How did the experience of teaching and learning from each other affect your relationship? Is this something you would like to integrate into your regular together time?

6. **Create a Routine**

   Make every effort to add this activity to your calendar once a week or at least one a month. This type of activity will create lasting memories and challenge you in ways your marriage may have yet to experience.

Benefits

- **Enhance Intellectual Intimacy**

  By sharing knowledge and skills, you not only learn from each other but also appreciate the depths of each other's intellect and curiosity.

- **Strengthens Connection**

  Engaging in mutual teaching and learning activities reinforces your bond and encourages collaboration and support.

- **Expands Horizons**

  This activity introduces new hobbies, skills, and knowledge into your lives, enriching your shared experiences and potentially discovering new common interests.

The goal of this activity is to celebrate the journey of learning with your partner, deepening your intellectual fidelity through shared curiosity, respect, and excitement for knowledge.

Day 26: Love and Respect

Do not let any unwholesome talk come out of your mouths, but only what is helpful for building others up according to their needs, that it may benefit those who listen.

Ephesians 4:29

Marriage is like a dance where every step, word, and action contributes to harmony or discord. Intellectual fidelity is the rhythm that keeps the dance fluid, valuing each other's thoughts and dreams and moving in sync with respect and understanding.

When dismissiveness or neglect disrupts this rhythm, it can lead to feeling trapped or undervalued. These moments signal the need for healing and reconnection. Like any dance, marriage requires both partners to be fully present, engaged, and supportive.

Take time to reflect: Are you moving in harmony, or are missteps causing you to stumble? Every conversation, shared dream, and action is a building block for your marriage. Choose wisely, with love and respect, to ensure your relationship remains strong and steady, no matter what storms come your way.

Daily Prayer

Heavenly Father,

We come before You today to ask for Your guidance and wisdom in our marriage. Help us to communicate with love, respect, and understanding. Teach us to value each other's thoughts, dreams, and feelings as we navigate life's challenges together. Remind us that our marriage reflects Your love and unity. Grant us the strength to build each other up, to face our challenges hand in hand, and to emerge stronger and more united in Your love. In Jesus' Name.

Amen.

Read: Chapter 10, Pages 212-217

Intellectual fidelity is as crucial as emotional and physical bonds in a marriage. When partners consistently dismiss or undervalue each other's thoughts and contributions, it leads to a breakdown in communication and mutual respect, culminating in a "breaking point" where one or both individuals feel emotionally and psychologically overwhelmed. This breaking point can manifest as withdrawal, sadness, or a decline in mental health, often exacerbated by the subtle nature of intellectual neglect, which might initially be dismissed as minor or temporary. The neglected partner may feel isolated, leading them to seek validation outside the marriage, which can spiral into further emotional detachment and potentially harmful behaviors.

🗝 Key Points

- **Subtlety of Intellectual Infidelity (Proverbs 14:29)**

  Intellectual neglect starts small but can lead to significant emotional distress, highlighting the importance of recognizing early signs of intellectual infidelity.

- **Manifestation of the Breaking Point (Psalm 34:18)**

  The neglected partner may experience emotional withdrawal or depression, signaling a deep-seated issue within the marriage that needs addressing.

- **Cycle of Misunderstanding (James 1:19)**

  The subtlety of intellectual neglect leads to a cycle of misunderstanding and resentment, underscoring the need for open communication.

- **Seeking External Validation (1 Timothy 5:8)**

  The neglected partner's search for acknowledgment outside the marriage underscores the importance of mutual respect and validation within the relationship. We will ultimately seek what we should find in our own homes elsewhere.

- **Path to Healing (Matthew 8:17)**

  Recognizing and addressing the root causes of intellectual infidelity and bringing Christ to the center can lead to healing and a stronger, more unified marriage.

✒ Personal Reflection

Reflect on how you have responded to your spouse's ideas or dreams. Have there been moments when your reactions were shaped by fear, insecurity, or stress rather than love and encouragement? Confess any tendencies to react defensively or dismissively, and consider how you can approach these conversations with greater openness and support, fostering trust and partnership in your marriage.

⟨⟩ Couple's Discussion

Talk about a recent time when one of you felt unheard or misunderstood. Share the emotions and thoughts that surfaced in that moment, and confess any frustrations, fears, or assumptions that may have contributed. Together, explore ways to improve communication and ensure you feel valued and respected, especially during difficult conversations. Consider creating regular check-ins or a simple way to signal when one of you feels misunderstood, neglected, dismissed, or overwhelmed.

Day 27: Intellectual Unity

If any of you lacks wisdom, you should ask God, who gives generously to all without finding fault, and it will be given to you.

James 1:5

Today, let us reflect on the "From Stronghold to Fortress" concept in our marriages. The transformation from a place of weakness to one of strength and unity requires active effort, understanding, and divine guidance. Intellectual infidelity, characterized by neglect or dismissiveness, can undermine the very foundation of our relationship. Yet, through God's wisdom and our commitment, we can turn these challenges into opportunities for growth and deeper connection.

Active listening is not merely a skill but an act of love, showing our partners that their thoughts and feelings are valued. Learning and sharing experiences can strengthen our bond and enhance our mutual respect. Prayer is crucial in seeking God's insight into our spouse's heart, leading to a deeper spiritual and intellectual connection. Celebrating each other's achievements reinforces mutual respect and encourages ongoing personal growth. Finally, seeking biblical counseling can provide valuable external perspectives and tools for nurturing intellectual fidelity.

As we journey through these principles, let us commit to transforming our marital challenges into opportunities for strengthening our bond, ensuring that our relationship becomes a fortress of love, respect, and mutual support.

📖 Daily Prayer

Heavenly Father,

We come before You today seeking Your wisdom and guidance in our marriage. Please help us to listen to each other actively and value and respect our spouse's thoughts and feelings. Teach us to learn together, share our passions, and grow in unity. Grant us the humility to seek Your insight through prayer, deepening our connection with each other and with You. Please help us to celebrate each other's successes, fostering an environment of mutual respect and encouragement. Guide us as we seek counseling and Your Word to strengthen our bond. May our marriage be a testament to Your love and a fortress of intellectual and spiritual unity, in Jesus' Name.

Amen.

📖 Read: Chapter 10, Pages 217-228

The concept of intellectual fidelity in marriage emphasizes the importance of mutual respect, understanding, and active engagement in each other's thoughts and ideas. It is about transforming neglected or misunderstood intellectual connections into strong, supportive unions. By actively listening, learning together, praying for insight, celebrating achievements, and seeking biblical counseling, couples can address and heal from intellectual infidelity. These actions foster a deeper emotional and spiritual bond, turning potential strongholds of conflict into fortresses of mutual support and intellectual unity, thereby strengthening the marriage.

🔑 Key Points

- **Active Listening (Proverbs 18:2)**
  Active listening is not just about hearing words but understanding the emotions and thoughts behind them. This approach fosters a deeper connection and trust, as it shows genuine interest and care for the partner's feelings and ideas, strengthening the marital bond.

- **Learning Together (Romans 12:10)**
  Engaging in shared educational activities or exploring each other's interests can significantly enhance intellectual intimacy. This mutual investment in learning broadens individual horizons and creates a shared space for growth and discovery, reinforcing the partnership.

- **Pray for Insight (James 1:5)**
  Prayer for understanding in your spouse's perspective invites divine wisdom into the relationship, promoting empathy and deeper connection. By seeking God's guidance, couples can navigate misunderstandings with grace and develop a more profound spiritual and intellectual bond.

- **Celebrate Achievements (Hebrews 10:24-25)**
  Acknowledging and celebrating each other's intellectual and personal achievements reinforces the value and respect each partner holds for the other. This practice not only boosts self-esteem and motivation but also strengthens the couple's unity and appreciation for each other's unique contributions.

- **Seek Biblical Counseling (Ephesians 4:2-3)**
  When facing challenges, professional guidance grounded in biblical principles can provide couples with new perspectives and strategies for overcoming intellectual barriers. Counseling offers a safe space to explore issues, learn effective communication skills, and rebuild the intellectual and emotional connection based on mutual respect and understanding.

🪶 Personal Reflection

Take a moment to examine your spouse's intellectual interests and passions. How intentional have you been in learning about and engaging with these areas? Identify one practical step you could take to improve your understanding and appreciation of their interests. Consider how this effort could strengthen your intellectual connection and deepen mutual respect.

_____
_____
_____
_____
_____
_____
_____
_____

💍 Couple's Discussion

Discuss the role of 'Active Listening' in your relationship. Share moments when you felt truly heard by your spouse and times when you felt overlooked or misunderstood. Confess any struggles with distraction, impatience, or assumptions that may have hindered deep listening. Reflect on how these experiences have impacted your emotional connection and trust. Together, establish new commitments or strategies to improve active listening, ensuring that both of you feel valued and understood in future conversations.

Day 28: A New Beginning

Finally, brothers and sisters, whatever is true, whatever is noble, whatever is right, whatever is pure, whatever is lovely, whatever is admirable—if anything is excellent or praiseworthy—think about such things.

Philippians 4:8

As we reflect on the journey through intellectual fidelity, Philippians 4:8 serves as a powerful light, guiding us towards a marriage rooted in the pursuit of all that is noble and pure. Intellectual fidelity is not merely about intellectual agreement or shared interests; it is about cultivating a shared space where the mind is encouraged to seek truth, beauty, and righteousness.

In this shared quest, we learn to appreciate the depth of our partner's thoughts, perspectives, and insights. We embark on a path where learning and growing together becomes an act of love, a testament to our commitment to each other and to the values we hold dear. Intellectual fidelity challenges us to engage deeply with the world and with each other, bringing to our marriage a richness that is both thought-provoking and soul-enriching.

As we close this chapter on intellectual fidelity, let us carry forward the lessons learned. Let us continue to inspire each other, challenge each other, and support each other in our mutual pursuit of wisdom and growth. In doing so, we build a marriage that not only withstands the test of time but also reflects the light and love of Christ in every conversation, decision, and moment shared.

📖 Daily Prayer

Heavenly Father,

As we conclude our exploration of intellectual fidelity, we thank You for the wisdom and insight You have imparted upon us. Guide us to always seek the truth, beauty, and goodness in our relationship and in the world around us. Help us to appreciate and nurture each other's intellect, fostering a marriage that glorifies You through mutual respect, love, and understanding. May our conversations be filled with kindness and our thoughts with purity, as we strive to reflect Your love in all aspects of our union. Empower us to carry these principles into every day of our marriage, enriching our bond and drawing us closer to You.

In Jesus' mighty name, Amen.

🪶 Personal Reflection

Think about the intellectual discussions and activities you shared with your spouse this week. Were there moments where you could have engaged more deeply? Identify one way to foster more meaningful intellectual connections moving forward.

_____

_____

_____

_____

_____

_____

_____

_____

_____

_____

💍 Couple's Discussion

Talk about how intellectual fidelity has shown up in your relationship this week. Share ways you have contributed to an environment of respect and curiosity and moments where you may have struggled to do so. Confess any habits of dismissing or neglecting each other's thoughts, and reflect on how that has affected your connection. Discuss new activities or discussions inspired by this week's readings that could deepen your intellectual bond. Explore how intentionally engaging in learning and meaningful conversations together can strengthen your marriage moving forward.

WEEK FIVE: FINANCIAL FIDELITY

Day 29: Financial Fidelity

The wise store up choice food and olive oil,
but fools gulp theirs down.

Proverbs 21:20

Let us take a moment to reflect on the biblical principle of stewardship, particularly in the context of marriage. Stewardship is not only about managing our finances wisely, but it is also about recognizing that everything we have is a gift from God. This includes our time, talents, and treasures. In marriage, this stewardship takes on a deeper dimension as we are called to manage these gifts individually and jointly with our spouse. Doing this can strengthen our marital bond, align our financial goals with God's will, and foster a deeper trust between partners. It is essential to remember that financial fidelity in marriage reflects our faithfulness to God. By managing our resources wisely and transparently, we honor God and build a stronger, more trusting relationship with our spouse.

📖 Daily Prayer

Heavenly Father,

Thank You for entrusting us with Your resources. Help us to manage them wisely, reflecting Your love and faithfulness in our marriage. Teach us to communicate openly with our spouse about our finances, make decisions together, and use our resources to honor You and strengthen our bond. Guide us in the path of financial fidelity so that our marriage may be a testament to Your providence and love, in Jesus' name.

Amen.

📖 Read: Chapter 11, Pages 229-234

The biblical concept of stewardship emphasizes the responsible management of resources, a principle that extends deeply into the fabric of a marital relationship. This stewardship entails not only the wise and sustainable use of material goods, as highlighted in Genesis 1:28, but also encompasses the nurturing of trust, transparency, and mutual respect between spouses, as illustrated in the Parable of the Talents (Matthew 25:14-30). Financial fidelity within marriage, therefore, is not merely about prudent budgeting or saving but is deeply rooted in the shared commitment to honor God's provisions and each other's needs. This approach fosters a stronger, more unified partnership, aligning both financial and spiritual goals. Conversely, financial infidelity, marked by secrecy and unilateral decision-making, undermines this unity, leading to mistrust and a weakening of the marital bond. Addressing these challenges requires a return to biblical principles, emphasizing open communication, mutual respect, and a collective approach to financial management.

🗝 Key Points

- **Stewardship and Responsibility (Genesis 1:28)**

  In marriage, this stewardship translates into jointly managing household finances and making decisions that reflect personal needs and the well-being of the family and the broader community. It is about recognizing that all resources are God-given and should be used to honor Him, including making ethical, sustainable decisions that reflect God's stewardship mandate.

- **Accountability and Growth (Matthew 25:14-30)**

  This parable serves as a metaphor for the stewardship of all gifts, including financial resources, within a marriage. It suggests that couples should preserve and seek to grow their resources responsibly. This growth is both economic and spiritual and relational, as couples work together, assess their progress, and hold each other accountable in love and respect.

- **Fidelity and Integrity (1 Corinthians 4:2)**

  In the context of marriage, this means being transparent about financial dealings and sharing information about income, debts, and expenditures. It involves making joint decisions on investments and expenditures, ensuring that both partners adhere to agreed-upon financial goals and principles, thus maintaining integrity in financial matters as a reflection of their commitment to each other and to God.

- **Wisdom and Prudence (Proverbs 21:20)**

  This wisdom extends beyond mere frugality to encompass discerning investment in the relationship's health and future. It involves creating and adhering to a budget, saving for unforeseen circumstances, and making informed decisions that secure the couple's financial future while also enabling generosity and support for others in need, reflecting the biblical values of stewardship and compassion.

- **Mutual Respect and Unity (Romans 12:10)**

In financial matters, this means involving each other in financial planning, respecting each other's viewpoints, and making decisions that benefit the marital partnership. It underscores the importance of building a financial plan that honors each person's goals and dreams, fostering a spirit of unity and mutual support that mirrors the biblical call to love and honor one another.

Personal Reflection

Assess your attitudes and actions around financial management in your marriage. Are there areas where you need to grow in transparency, generosity, or wisdom? Consider how your financial choices affect your family, community, and relationship with God.

_____
_____
_____
_____
_____
_____
_____
_____
_____

Couple's Discussion

Talk with your spouse about how you both currently handle financial management and stewardship. Confess any fears, frustrations, or struggles you have had in this area, and reflect on whether your financial decisions reflect trust, respect, and alignment with God's principles. Identify any changes you need to make and set specific goals that honor God and strengthen unity in your marriage. Pray together for wisdom and guidance in managing your resources with faithfulness and integrity.

Day 30: Financial Unity

For the husband is the head of the wife as Christ is the head of the church, his body, of which he is the Savior.

Ephesians 5:23

Financial stewardship is a vital responsibility in marriage. Financial infidelity—hidden purchases, secret accounts, or unilateral decisions—can deeply damage trust and unity. The story of Ananias and Sapphira reminds us of the importance of honesty and integrity, especially in financial matters. Transparency and mutual respect are essential to building a strong foundation.

Biblical headship calls for leading with love, serving with humility, and managing resources wisely, as Joseph did during Egypt's famine. This means making decisions that prioritize the well-being of the family, fostering cooperation and trust.

By aligning your financial decisions with God's design, you strengthen your bond as a couple and reflect Christ's love and unity. Let your financial stewardship be an act of faithfulness, building trust and fostering a spirit of mutual respect in your marriage.

Daily Prayer

Heavenly Father,

We come before You today seeking wisdom and guidance in our financial stewardship. Help us to recognize and address any form of financial infidelity in our marriage. Grant us the courage to maintain transparency with our spouse and to make decisions that honor You and strengthen our union. Teach us to embody the biblical principles of headship and partnership, leading with love and serving with humility. May our financial decisions reflect our trust in Your provision and our commitment to each other. In Jesus' name.

Amen.

Read: Chapter 11, Pages 234-240

This explores the detrimental effects of financial infidelity within a marriage, highlighting various forms such as hidden purchases, secret accounts, and unilateral financial decisions. It underscores the importance of transparency, mutual respect, and shared decision-making in financial matters as fundamental to maintaining trust and integrity in a marital relationship. The biblical perspective emphasizes stewardship, honesty, and the responsible management of resources entrusted by God. The narrative also discusses the concept of headship in financial matters, advocating for a leadership style that mirrors Christ's love and service, guided by biblical teachings.

Key Points

- **Transparency and Mutual Respect (Matthew 25:14-30)**

  In a marriage, transparency about financial matters fosters a climate of trust and mutual respect, which are cornerstones of a strong relationship. When both partners are open about their spending, earnings, and financial strategies, it eliminates suspicions and builds a foundation of honesty, reflecting the accountability and responsible resource management highlighted in the Parable of the Talents.

- **Shared Decision-Making (Philippians 2:3-4)**

  Engaging in shared decision-making reinforces the partnership aspect of marriage, ensuring that both individuals have a voice in financial matters. This collaborative approach not only aligns with the biblical mandate for stewardship and dominion over resources but also strengthens the marital bond by valuing each partner's perspective and contributions, fostering unity and mutual respect.

- **Stewardship and Accountability (1 Corinthians 4:2, Proverbs 21:20)**

  Effective stewardship involves more than just careful budgeting; it encompasses a commitment to ethical and responsible financial management. By holding each other accountable and making decisions that reflect integrity and wisdom, couples honor God's provisions and demonstrate their commitment to His principles, as outlined in scriptures like 1 Corinthians 4:2 and Proverbs 21:20, which advocate for wise and honest handling of resources.

- **Biblical Headship in Finances (Ephesians 5:23)**

  True biblical headship in financial matters is characterized by leadership that prioritizes the well-being and security of the family, reflecting Christ's sacrificial love for the Church. This approach involves consulting one's spouse, making decisions that benefit the entire family, and leading by example in stewardship, thereby embodying the protective, service-oriented leadership demonstrated by Joseph in Genesis during Egypt's famine.

- **Consequences of Financial Deceit (Acts 5:1-11)**

  The story of Ananias and Sapphira serves as a stark reminder of the serious consequences of financial deceit, not just between individuals but within the broader community of believers. Their fate underscores the importance of honesty and transparency in all dealings, particularly financial ones, as deceit not only undermines personal integrity but also the trust and unity foundational to both marriage and the Christian community.

🪶 Personal Reflection

Think about your financial behaviors: Have you ever hidden purchases, debts, or financial details from your spouse? Confess any fears that may have impacted trust or financial health in your relationship and consider how to rebuild openness and accountability.

_____

_____

_____

_____

_____

_____

_____

_____

💍 Couple's Discussion

Discuss your individual and shared beliefs about financial transparency and decision-making. Confess any fears, past experiences, or misunderstandings that may have led to financial decisions being made in isolation. Explore how you can improve communication, establish shared financial goals, and ensure both of you feel involved and respected. Reflect on how biblical principles of stewardship, honesty, and shared responsibility can guide your financial unity moving forward.

Day 31: Small Things

Honor the Lord with your wealth,
with the firstfruits of all your crops;
¹⁰ then your barns will be filled to overflowing,
and your vats will brim over with new wine.

Proverbs 3:9-10

Our financial habits in marriage reveal our values, fears, and trust in God. Proverbs 3:9-10 reminds us that honoring God with our wealth is a spiritual discipline, encouraging generosity, responsible stewardship, and trust in His provision. Managing finances wisely is more than planning—it is worship, showing reliance on God and commitment to each other.

Financial faithfulness means making decisions that reflect shared values and align with God's guidance. This journey requires open communication, mutual understanding, and, sometimes, sacrifices. These challenges create opportunities for deeper intimacy and unity as you support each other's goals, share burdens, and celebrate successes.

As you honor God with your finances, remember that your true treasure lies in the love you share and the life you build together under His grace. Let your financial faithfulness testify to your trust in God and your commitment to each other.

📖 Daily Prayer

Heavenly Father,

We come before You today seeking wisdom and guidance in managing the resources You have entrusted to us. Help us to honor You with our wealth, making decisions that reflect Your love and generosity. Teach us to communicate openly about our financial dreams and fears, and to find common ground that honors both our needs and Your will. May our financial choices strengthen our bond, deepen our trust in You, and serve as a beacon of Your love and provision.

In Jesus' name, we pray, Amen.

👫 Fidelity Builder: Mini-Budgets

This builder aims to initiate open dialogue about financial priorities, aligning small, everyday expenses with biblical values in giving, stewardship, personal growth, and joy and pleasure. This activity is meant to be a practical and manageable start towards integrating biblical principles into your daily financial decisions, fostering open communication and mutual understanding in financial matters.

Instructions:

1. **Prepare Your Materials**

    Each partner will need a set of small notes (like Post-its) and a pen. Access to your current budget or financial statements can provide clarity and realism to the exercise.

2. **Pray for Guidance**

    Begin with a short prayer, asking for God's wisdom and discernment to align your financial decisions with His will and values.

3. **Write Your Priorities**
    - Independently, each partner writes down three small-scale expenses (or wishes for expenses) on separate notes for each of the following biblical categories:
        - **Giving:** Tithing, charitable donations, etc.
        - **Stewardship:** Debt payments, savings, etc.
        - **Personal Growth:** Educational books, courses, seminars, etc.
        - **Joy and Pleasure:** Dining out, movie nights, hobbies, etc.
    - Below each description, write a realistic monthly budget for that item.

4. **Share and Align**
    - Take turns sharing your notes, explaining why each expense is essential to you and how you believe it aligns with biblical principles.
    - If you have duplicates, those should be prioritized.
    - Discuss discrepancies in your perceptions or priorities, striving to understand each other's viewpoints.

5. **Create a Joint Mini-Budget**
    - From the items shared, select one from each category that you both agree to prioritize in your monthly budget.
    - Discuss how these chosen expenses reflect your shared values and goals as a couple.

6. **Display and Commit**
    - Place the agreed-upon notes in a visible area, like on the refrigerator or a bulletin board, as a reminder of your mutual commitments.
    - Commit to reviewing these priorities at the end of each week. Discuss how well you adhered to them, what adjustments might be needed, and whether any new small-scale expenses should be considered for the next month.
    - Each month, picking a day that makes sense and putting it on the calendar, pick a new item from the list and add it to your budge. Repeat this every month until all the items are included. If you think of more, add to the shared list.

Reflection

After sharing and deciding on your joint mini budget, reflect on:
- How did this activity affect your understanding of each other's financial values and priorities?
- How do these small-scale financial decisions reflect your shared vision for a life aligned with God's principles?

Day 32: United Headship

Plans fail for lack of counsel,
but with many advisers they succeed.

Proverbs 15:22

In the journey of marriage, particularly in the realm of finances, the temptation to assume unilateral control can be strong, especially under the guise of headship. However, true biblical headship involves partnership, mutual respect, and shared decision-making. It is a dance of balance, where both partners contribute their unique perspectives and wisdom to navigate the family's financial waters. This approach not only aligns with God's design for marriage but also fortifies the marital bond against the storms of life.

When one partner takes on the financial burden alone, it can lead to a host of issues: pride, secrecy, impulsivity, and misplaced priorities, which can destabilize the family's financial and emotional well-being. Conversely, when spouses engage in open communication, respect each other's insights, and make decisions together, they embody the unity and mutual submission depicted in Ephesians 5:21. This shared journey fosters a deeper trust and partnership, reflecting Christ's relationship with the Church.

Today, let us reflect on the dynamics of financial decision-making in our marriages. Are we embodying the principles of shared sumbission and mutual respect? Are we inviting our spouse into the financial conversation, valuing their input and wisdom? Let us strive to build a financial partnership that honors God and strengthens our marital bond.

Daily Prayer

Heavenly Father,

We thank You for the gift of marriage and the partnership it represents. Guide us in our financial decisions to reflect Your wisdom and unity. Help us to avoid the pitfalls of pride, secrecy, and impulsivity, and instead foster open communication, mutual respect, and shared decision-making with our spouse. Remind us that true headship mirrors Christ's love and leadership, serving and valuing the other above oneself. Strengthen our marriage bond, Lord, and lead us to financial decisions that honor You and benefit our family. In Jesus' name.

Amen.

📖 Read: Chapter 11, Pages 241-246

In this part of chapter 11 we the concept of financial infidelity and its detrimental effects on marriage, emphasizing the importance of mutual decision-making and transparency. It highlights various forms of financial deceit, such as hidden purchases and secret accounts, which can undermine trust and lead to emotional and spiritual strain. The biblical perspective on headship is discussed, advocating for a partnership approach in financial matters, reflecting mutual respect and shared responsibilities. The narrative underscores the need for aligning financial decisions with biblical principles, seeking God's wisdom, and the importance of both spouses actively participating in financial planning and management.

🔑 Key Points

- **Pride and Self-Reliance in Headship (Proverbs 16:18)**

    The text discusses how unilateral decision-making in financial matters can lead to pride and self-reliance, distancing one from the collaborative and consultative approach intended in marriage. This behavior contradicts the wisdom of seeking collective counsel and admitting one's limitations, as advised in Proverbs 16:18.

- **Secrecy, Dishonesty, and Impulsivity (James 1:5, Proverbs 15:22)**

    It highlights the dangers of secrecy and dishonesty in financial management within a marriage, leading to distrust and conflict. The text encourages seeking God's wisdom in decision-making to avoid impulsive actions, aligning with the guidance provided in James 1:5 and Proverbs 15:22.

- **Shared Financial Decision-Making (Matthew 6:21)**

    The importance of shared decision-making in financial matters is emphasized, reflecting mutual respect and unity. This approach prevents the pitfalls of misplaced priorities and ensures that materialistic desires do not overshadow family needs or spiritual directives, as reminded in Matthew 6:21.

- **The Role of Wives in Financial Affairs (Proverbs 31)**

The text underlines the significant role wives play in financial management, challenging the notion of exclusive male headship in financial decisions. It suggests that wives should be actively involved and respected in financial planning, drawing on the example of the virtuous woman in Proverbs 31.

- **Biblical Model of Marriage and Financial Unity**

    Finally, the text argues for a marriage model based on unity, mutual respect, and joint decision-making, mirroring the relationship between Christ and the Church. It warns against the detrimental effects of ignoring a spouse's input in financial matters, advocating for a partnership that reflects the biblical blueprint for marriage.

Personal Reflection

Evaluate your communication about finances with your spouse. Have you been secretive, dishonest, or avoidant in any way? Confess where your actions may not align with the biblical call for transparency and honesty, and consider how to foster greater openness moving forward.

_____
_____
_____
_____
_____
_____

Couple's Discussion

Talk about how you can improve financial decision-making to make it more balanced, transparent, and inclusive. Confess any struggles with control, fear, or passivity in financial matters, and reflect on how mutual submission and headship (Ephesians 5:21, Genesis 2:24) apply to your approach. Discuss how you can create a financial strategy that honors both perspectives, and consider setting regular times to review finances together to ensure unity and respect in every decision.

Day 33: Sharing Stewardship

Keep your lives free from the love of money and be content with what you have, because God has said,

"Never will I leave you;

never will I forsake you."

Hebrews 13:5

Today, let us reflect on the essence of biblical stewardship and financial headship within the context of marriage. It is not merely about budgeting, saving, or investing wisely, but about aligning these activities with God's will and teachings. The biblical approach to finances is a holistic one, integrating spiritual, relational, and material aspects. It emphasizes the importance of mutual decision-making, transparency, and shared goals between spouses, reflecting the unity and partnership intended by God. As we manage our resources, we are called to remember that everything we own is entrusted to us by God, not for our benefit alone but for the advancement of His kingdom. This perspective transforms our financial practices into acts of worship and avenues for ministry.

📖 Daily Prayer

Heavenly Father,

We thank You for the resources You have entrusted to us. Help us to manage them wisely, not as isolated individuals but as united partners in marriage, reflecting Your love and stewardship. Grant us the wisdom to make decisions that honor You, the courage to seek and heed godly counsel, and the generosity to share Your blessings with others. May our financial practices reflect our commitment to You and contribute to the growth of Your kingdom. Teach us to find contentment in Your provision and to remember that our true treasure is found in You. In Jesus' name.

Amen.

📖 Read: Chapter 11, Pages 246-254

The text underscores the importance of incorporating biblical principles into financial management and stewardship within a marriage. This aims to create a harmonious and prosperous household that aligns with God's teachings. It discusses the significance of budgeting, planning, generosity, investing in family, seeking wisdom, and teaching the next generation as key aspects of effective financial management. The narrative further delves into the transition from individual headship to collective stewardship. It stresses the importance of couples working together to manage resources wisely, make informed decisions, and contribute to the growth of God's Kingdom. The text highlights the necessity of transparency, mutual respect, and shared decision-making to achieve oneness in marriage, particularly in financial matters. This ensures not only financial security but also spiritual and relational harmony.

🗝 Key Points

- **Budgeting and Planning (Proverbs 21:5)**

  The text underscores the importance of proactive financial planning and saving, drawing parallels with biblical narratives that advocate for foresight and preparation. It suggests that just as biblical figures anticipated future events and acted wisely, couples should also plan for future needs and save accordingly to ensure stability during challenging times.

- **Generosity and Investment (2 Corinthians 9:6-7)**

  Highlighting the value of generosity, the narrative encourages sharing God's blessings with others and investing in the family's future, such as through education or family businesses. It reflects the biblical principle that true wealth comes from God and should be used to bless others and secure the family's long-term well-being.

- **Seeking Wisdom and Guidance (Proverbs 15:22)**

  Stressing the need for counsel and collective wisdom, the text advises couples to consult with financial advisors and involve family members in financial decisions. This approach aligns with biblical teachings that advocate for seeking guidance and multiple perspectives to ensure well-informed and balanced decisions.

- **Teaching and Guiding (Proverbs 22:6)**

  The narrative emphasizes the role of parents (and grandparents) in educating the next generation about financial stewardship, hard work, and wise decision-making. It suggests that imparting these values and skills is crucial for raising responsible and God-honoring stewards.

- **Oneness in Financial Decisions (Ephesians 5:21)**

    The text calls for unity and partnership in financial headship and stewardship, advocating for a collaborative approach to financial management within marriage. It highlights the importance of transparency, shared goals, and mutual respect, ensuring that both partners contribute to and agree on financial decisions, reflecting the biblical model of marriage as a partnership.

Personal Reflection

Evaluate your personal feelings towards money and resources. Do you find yourself leaning more towards fear and hoarding, or do you feel a sense of trust and generosity? How does this impact your financial decisions and your relationship with your spouse or family?

_____
_____
_____
_____
_____
_____

Couple's Discussion

Discuss together how you can implement or improve upon the principles of biblical headship and stewardship in your financial life. Consider creating a unified plan that includes setting a budget, planning for the future, being generous, avoiding unnecessary debt, and seeking wise counsel. Reflect on how these changes could enhance not only your financial security but also your spiritual growth and relationship with each other and with God.

Day 34: Restoration

I am not saying this because I am in need, for I have learned to be content whatever the circumstances. ¹² I know what it is to be in need, and I know what it is to have plenty. I have learned the secret of being content in any and every situation, whether well fed or hungry, whether living in plenty or in want. ¹³ I can do all this through him who gives me strength.

Philippians 4:11-13

Let us see how Jesus' forgiveness and love can change our lives by looking at the story of Zacchaeus. His story shows us that financial integrity is not just about numbers, but also about our hearts and our commitment to God. We should use our money to serve God and others, not just ourselves. Let us ask ourselves some questions: Are we using our resources to help others in need? Are we content with what we have? Are we seeking God's guidance in our financial decisions? By aligning our financial practices with God's principles, we can cultivate a heart that finds joy in giving, contentment in what we have, and wisdom in our decisions. Let us honor God and help others with our finances.

Daily Prayer

Heavenly Father,

Once again, we thank You for Your endless grace and for the lessons You teach us through Your Word. Help us to have a heart like Zacchaeus, ready to make things right and to live generously. Grant us the wisdom to manage the resources You have entrusted to us in a way that honors You. Teach us contentment in every circumstance and guide me in balancing generosity with enjoyment of Your blessings. May our actions and decisions reflect Your love and contribute to the building of Your Kingdom. In Jesus' name.

Amen.

Read: Chapter 11, Pages 254-262

Financial infidelity can estrange individuals from their spiritual communities and from Christ, emphasizing the need for a repentant heart and a desire for restoration within the Christian fellowship. True restoration involves more than just rectifying financial wrongs; it requires a genuine transformation of the heart and a commitment to live righteously, as demonstrated by Zacchaeus's story in Luke 19:1-10. This narrative illustrates that genuine repentance leads to actions that restore relationships with both God and the community. Financial stewardship within a marriage should reflect a partnership aligned with biblical teachings, promoting transparency, mutual decision-making, and a shared commitment to God's kingdom. This approach not only secures financial stability but also fosters spiritual growth and communal well-being, showcasing a life transformed by God's grace and guided by His principles.

🗝 Key Points

- **Restoration through Repentance (Luke 19:8-9)**

    Financial infidelity can alienate individuals from their spiritual community and from Christ. True restoration involves more than rectifying financial errors; it requires a repentant heart seeking a deeper relationship with Christ and reintegration into His community, as illustrated by Zacchaeus's transformation in Luke.

- **Impact of Generosity (2 Corinthians 9:6-7)**

    Generosity is a key aspect of financial restoration and stewardship. It is not just about giving away wealth but about a change of heart that leads to actions reflecting justice, generosity, and a restored relationship with both God and the community.

- **Balancing Benevolence and Enjoyment (1 Timothy 6:6-10)**

    The Scriptures provide guidance on managing finances that balance the act of giving with the rightful enjoyment of God's blessings. This balance is crucial for living a life that honors God while also enjoying the fruits of one's labor.

- **Stewardship and Contentment (Ecclesiastes 5:18-19)**

    Financial stewardship in a marriage involves managing resources wisely, with a focus on generosity, prudence, and contentment. This approach aligns with biblical teachings and ensures that financial decisions honor God and support the well-being of the broader community. But this does not me God intends us to live a life of joyless suffering. It is good to discover happiness, and we should treasure it, for it glorifies God.

- **Unified Financial Vision in Marriage (Philippians 4:6-7)**

Achieving oneness in financial matters requires transparency, shared decision-making, and a commitment to mutual goals within the marriage. This unity in financial headship and stewardship reflects a more profound spiritual oneness and honors God's design for marriage.

🪶 Personal Reflection

Examine your heart regarding contentment: Does discontentment influence your financial decisions more than faith and trust in God's provision? Reflect on 1 Timothy 6:6-10 and confess any areas where your perspective on possessions or finances needs to align with His truth.

_____
_____
_____
_____
_____
_____
_____
_____

💍 Couple's Discussion

Talk about how you balance enjoying God's blessings with being faithful stewards of His resources. Confess any struggles with materialism, fear of lack, or reluctance to be generous. Discuss how you can cultivate both gratitude and a heart for giving, ensuring your financial decisions honor God and reflect His Kingdom values. Identify specific steps to live with joy and generosity in your marriage.

Day 35: Treasured Heart

For where your treasure is, there your heart will be also.

Matthew 6:21

Matthew 6:21 reminds us that where we invest our resources—time, energy, or finances—reveals our true priorities. In marriage, financial fidelity is more than budgeting; it reflects trust, shared values, and a commitment to honor God with your wealth.

Financial fidelity invites couples to align their resources with mutual goals and Christ's teachings. It is not about financial prosperity but about unity and purpose. Even routine tasks like budgeting become acts of worship and trust in God's provision, fostering generosity, stewardship, and contentment.

As you reflect on financial fidelity, consider how your financial decisions reflect your faith and shared vision. Let this journey deepen your unity and be a source of blessing to others. By placing your treasures and hearts in God's hands, you will find peace, joy, and a marriage anchored in eternal priorities by placing your treasures and hearts in God's hands.

📖 Daily Prayer

Lord,

As we reflect on the lessons of financial fidelity, guide our hearts and minds towards a deeper understanding of stewardship and generosity. Help us to see our finances through Your eyes, as tools for Your kingdom and as expressions of our love and commitment to each other. Strengthen our resolve to make financial decisions that honor You, promote unity within our marriage, and reflect our trust in Your provision. May our journey in financial fidelity deepen our relationship with You and with each other, manifesting Your love and grace in all that we do.

In Jesus' name, Amen.

🪶 Personal Reflection

Think about the financial goals you have set individually and as a couple. Do these goals reflect Christ-centered values like stewardship and generosity? Confess any ways your planning might stray from biblical principles and consider how to align them more closely with trust in God's provision.

_____
_____
_____
_____
_____
_____
_____
_____
_____
_____

💍 Couple's Discussion

Talk about how you can apply biblical principles of financial stewardship—tithing, saving, investing, and giving—into your daily life. Confess any fears or challenges you face in these areas and how they have impacted your marriage. Discuss ways to support each other in making financial decisions that honor God, strengthen your trust, and reflect His provision and purpose for your marriage.

WEEK SIX: EMOTIONAL FIDELITY

Day 36: Emotional Fidelity

Be kind and compassionate to one another, forgiving each other, just as in Christ God forgave you.

Ephesians 4:32

Today, reflect on the power of kindness, compassion, and forgiveness in your marriage. These qualities are not just niceties; they are the very fabric of a Christ-centered union. Your emotional well-being and the health of your marriage are deeply intertwined with how you treat each other, especially in moments of vulnerability and misunderstanding.

Consider the early influences on your emotional development and recognize how they may shape your reactions and interactions with your spouse. Acknowledge the role of past relationships and experiences but choose to live in the present, where grace abounds. Let the love you share be a testament to God's transformative power, reflecting His patience, understanding, and forgiveness.

As you move through your day, be intentional in your interactions. Offer words of affirmation, listen with empathy, and be present. Remember, emotional fidelity is not just about avoiding wrongs but actively doing right by your spouse, honoring them as God's precious gift to you.

📖 Daily Prayer

Heavenly Father,

Thank You for the gift of marriage and the journey of emotional growth it entails. Help me to understand Your love and compassion and let it guide my actions in my marriage. Heal the wounds of the past that hinder my emotional openness. Grant me the courage to be vulnerable and the grace to forgive as You have forgiven me. Strengthen our bond to reflect Your love and faithfulness, and remind us of Your mercy in moments of misunderstanding.

In Jesus' name, Amen.

📖 Read: Chapter 12, Pages 263-272

Our emotional health, shaped from childhood through various relationships, plays a crucial role in our ability to engage in deep, meaningful connections, particularly in marriage. Early experiences with family, friends, and romantic interests can significantly influence our capacity for vulnerability, trust, and empathy—key components of emotional fidelity in marriage. This fidelity reflects God's relational nature and is essential for a spiritually and emotionally fulfilling union. Emotional fidelity involves being present, supportive, and loyal, fostering a safe space for mutual growth and deeper understanding of God's love. It requires navigating the balance between personal enjoyment and collective benevolence, guided by principles of generosity, contentment, and self-sacrifice, as outlined in Scripture.

🔑 Key Points

- **Childhood Influences (Proverbs 22:6)**

  The emotional environment of our childhood, including parental relationships and early friendships, sets the foundation for our emotional development and affects our future relationships, including marriage. This verse exemplifies the importance of the emotional and spiritual environment in which children are raised. It highlights the long-term impact of childhood experiences on an individual's behavior and relationships, including marriage.

- **Importance of Vulnerability and Empathy (Ephesians 4:32)**

  In marriage, vulnerability allows for genuine intimacy, while empathy fosters a supportive and understanding relationship, both of which are crucial for maintaining emotional fidelity. Here Paul speaks to the heart of vulnerability and empathy within marriage. It calls for spouses to be open, understanding, and forgiving, mirroring the compassion and forgiveness of Christ, which are essential for genuine intimacy and a supportive relationship.

- **Spiritual and Emotional Reflection (1 John 4:7-8)**

  Our emotions and how we manage them in marriage reflect God's relational character. Emotional fidelity in marriage honors God's design and deepens our connection with Him. This passage emphasizes that our capacity to love and maintain emotional fidelity reflects our relationship with God. It reminds us that our emotional expressions in marriage should mirror God's love and relational nature.

- **Consequences of Emotional Infidelity (Hebrews 13:4)**

  Emotional infidelity, characterized by seeking emotional fulfillment outside of marriage, undermines trust and intimacy, leading to a weakened spiritual and emotional bond between spouses. While this verse directly addresses physical infidelity, it also underscores the broader principle of honoring marriage in all aspects, including emotional fidelity. Emotional infidelity, like physical, dishonors the sanctity of marriage and undermines the trust and intimacy between spouses.

- **Restoration and Growth (James 5:16)**
Addressing and healing from emotional infidelity or neglect involves fostering transparency, prioritizing the marital relationship, and aligning with biblical principles of love and forgiveness, thereby restoring the emotional and spiritual unity intended for marriage. The Apostle James highlights the path to healing and restoration in the wake of emotional infidelity or neglect. It emphasizes the importance of transparency, confession, and mutual support in the healing process, aligning with biblical principles of forgiveness and reconciliation to restore emotional and spiritual unity in marriage.

Personal Reflection

Think about your emotional contributions to your marriage. Are there ways you might be seeking fulfillment outside your relationship, even in non-romantic contexts? Confess any misaligned priorities and consider how you can redirect your energy to strengthen the emotional bond with your spouse.

_____
_____
_____
_____
_____
_____
_____

Couple's Discussion

Talk about how emotional fidelity is currently reflected in your marriage. Share moments when you felt deeply connected and supported, as well as times when you experienced emotional distance or neglect. Confess any fears, past wounds, or habits that may have contributed to disconnection. Together, explore ways to strengthen your emotional intimacy and commitment, ensuring that your marriage remains a place of trust, safety, and unwavering support.

Day 37: Bids of Affection

Therefore, as God's chosen people, holy and dearly loved, clothe yourselves with compassion, kindness, humility, gentleness and patience. ¹³ Bear with each other and forgive one another if any of you has a grievance against someone. Forgive as the Lord forgave you.

Colossians 3:12-13

In the journey of marriage, the significance of 'Bids of Affection' cannot be overstated. These small gestures—a touch, a glance, a word—serve as the heartbeat of our emotional connection with our spouse. They are the silent language of love, seeking reassurance and intimacy amid life's hustle. Just as Jesus responded to every bid for His attention with love and presence, we are called to mirror this divine attentiveness in our marriages.

Acknowledging and responding to these bids is an act of emotional faithfulness, a reflection of Christ's love that values and cherishes our partner. It is in these moments that we see the true essence of a Christ-centered marriage, where every gesture of affection is an opportunity to strengthen our bond and deepen our connection with God.

However, neglecting these bids can lead to a gradual erosion of the emotional fabric that binds our hearts together. This neglect, though not as conspicuous as outright betrayal, can create a void filled with loneliness and misunderstanding, distancing us from our spouse and from God's design for our union.

Today, let us commit to being more attentive to our spouse's bids for affection, seeing them as sacred invitations to connect and reinforce our marital bond. Let us strive to embody the responsive heart of Jesus, ensuring that our marriage reflects His deep, unconditional love.

📖 Daily Prayer

Heavenly Father,

Thank You for the gift of marriage and the joy of sharing life with my spouse. Help me cherish the small gestures of love we share and respond with the attentiveness and love of Christ. Teach me to be humble and gentle and to prioritize our connection. Let our marriage reflect Your faithfulness and grow stronger, rooted in Your love and wisdom.

Amen.

📖 Read: Chapter 12, Pages 272-277

In general, in relationships, and for marriage in particular, the concept of "Bids of Affection" plays a pivotal role in fostering a deep, emotional connection between partners. These bids, encompassing small gestures of love and attention, are foundational to building and maintaining the emotional health of a relationship. Ignoring these bids can lead to a gradual erosion of intimacy, fostering loneliness and misunderstanding, while responding to them strengthens the bond, mirroring Christ's attentive and loving nature. The text underscores the importance of these interactions in maintaining emotional fidelity, a commitment that extends beyond avoiding betrayal to actively nurturing closeness, trust, and mutual support. It highlights the necessity of vulnerability, empathy, and intimacy in creating a safe emotional space, allowing couples to share their innermost thoughts and feelings, thereby deepening their connection with each other and with God. The narrative also delves into the challenges that arise when these emotional bids are neglected, leading to a void filled by misunderstanding and hurt, and emphasizes the importance of recognizing and responding to these bids to foster a spiritually profound and emotionally fulfilling marriage.

🔑 Key Points

- **Importance of Bids of Affection (Colossians 3:12-14)**
  The text emphasizes the significance of small gestures and overtures, termed as "bids of affection," in maintaining and nurturing the emotional connection between spouses. These bids, which can be as simple as a touch, a glance, or a word, are crucial for building intimacy and ensuring a strong, Christ-centered marriage.

- **Emotional Fidelity and Christ's Example (1 Peter 3:8-9)**
  The concept of emotional fidelity is highlighted as being central to a healthy marriage, with Jesus Christ's attentive and loving responses to those around Him serving as the ultimate model. Couples are encouraged to reflect Christ's character by recognizing and responding to their partner's bids for affection, thereby strengthening their emotional bond and unity.

- **Consequences of Neglecting Bids of Affection (Ephesians 4:31-32)**
  Ignoring or overlooking these bids can lead to emotional infidelity, characterized not by outright betrayal but by a gradual erosion of the couple's emotional connection. This neglect can result in feelings of loneliness, misunderstanding, and hurt, damaging the spiritual and emotional closeness intended in marriage.

- **Recognizing and Responding to Bids (James 1:19)**

The text outlines various types of bids, including verbal, physical, and requests for attention or involvement, and stresses the importance of acknowledging and responding to these bids to build emotional intimacy and trust. Failure to do so can lead to a disconnection and undermine the relationship's foundation. Often these bids can be misunderstood through lends of trauma or false vows, it is critical we take our time to understand them through our spouse's eyes.

- **Loneliness and Reconnection (Hebrews 10:24-25)**

The narrative illustrates how the busyness of family life and other responsibilities can create an emotional distance between spouses, leading to a form of loneliness that stems from a lack of intimate connection. It underscores the need for couples to reevaluate their priorities and make concerted efforts to reconnect and address the emotional voids in their marriage, thereby preventing the relationship from becoming a shell of its intended design.

Personal Reflection

Think about the past week: Were there moments when your spouse extended a 'bid for affection'? How did you respond? Confess any times you may have overlooked their efforts and consider how you can respond more attentively and lovingly in the future.

_____
_____
_____
_____
_____
_____
_____
_____

Couple's Discussion

Share a recent moment when one of you felt a bid for affection was ignored or overlooked. Confess how it affected your emotions and connection in that moment. Together, discuss ways to become more attentive and responsive to each other's needs, ensuring that your marriage remains a place of emotional security and love.

Day 38: With Love

We love because he first loved us.

1 John 4:19

Love is the divine thread that binds us, reflecting God's love poured into our hearts. As 1 John 4:19 reminds us, our ability to love comes from God's steadfast, sacrificial, and selfless love. This love is more than a feeling; it is a commitment, an action, and a choice.

In marriage, love means choosing understanding, empathy, and vulnerability every day. It is about seeing your spouse through the lens of grace, building trust, and creating a safe space for shared fears and dreams. God's love challenges us to weave kindness, forgiveness, and support into our relationship, reflecting Christ's love to our spouse.

As you journey through life together, strive to deepen your understanding of God's love, embody its principles, and share its grace. Let your marriage be a testament to the transformative power of divine love, a source of strength and hope for each other.

📖 Daily Prayer

Lord,

We are in awe of Your unconditional love. Help us reflect that love in our marriage, showing patience, kindness, and understanding, even in challenges. Teach us to communicate openly, support each other, and celebrate life's joys together.

May our marriage be a testimony of Your love, grounded in divine principles. Bless us with wisdom and strength to build a relationship that flourishes in love, joy, and peace, always reflecting Your grace in every word and action.

Amen.

👫 Fidelity Builder: A Love Letter

This activity aims to deepen emotional intimacy and understanding between partners by writing love letters that express feelings, appreciation, and commitment. This exercise not only reinforces the bond of emotional fidelity but also serves as a tangible reminder of your love and commitment to each other. This is an opportunity to express love, appreciation, and affirmation, not exchange grievances.

Instructions:

1. **Prepare Your Space**

   Set aside a quiet, comfortable space where each of you can reflect and write without distractions. Consider setting the mood with soft music or lighting to encourage openness and vulnerability. If you have any special music (wedding song, worship, etc.), be sure to add that to the play list.

2. **Prayer for Guidance**

   Begin with a short prayer together, asking God to guide your thoughts and words and allow His love to flow through your letters.

3. **Writing Your Letter**

   Each partner takes a piece of paper or opens a new document on a digital device. Start by reflecting on the following prompts to guide your writing:

   - **Intimacy:** Share something your partner has done recently that made you feel loved and cherished. Describe why it was meaningful to you.
   - **Vulnerability:** Open about a fear or worry you have been carrying and explain how your partner's support can make a difference.
   - **Empathy:** Acknowledge a challenge your partner has faced and express your understanding and solidarity.
   - **Gratitude:** List at least three qualities you admire in your partner and thank them for specific instances where these qualities were a blessing to you.
   - **Commitment:** Reaffirm your commitment to supporting and loving your partner, mentioning how you plan to grow together in Christ.

4. **Exchange and Read**

   Once both partners have finished writing, exchange letters. Take turns reading each other's letters in silence. Allow yourselves to fully absorb the words and feelings expressed.

5. **Discuss**

   After reading, discuss your letters. Share how writing and reading the letters felt, what surprised you, and how it made you feel about your partner and your relationship.

6. **Prayer of Thanksgiving**

Conclude with a prayer together, thanking God for the gift of each other and asking for His guidance in continuing to build emotional fidelity in your marriage.

7. **Make it a Habit.**

This exercise may feel a bit awkward, but this is the type of regular communication spouses need to feel loved, appreciated, and connected. These letters are way to share and articulate your emotional life with each other as you learn to understand and communicate them more fluently in person.

Tips for Writing Your Letter:

- **Be Genuine:** Write from the heart. Your partner knows you and will appreciate sincerity over perfection.
- **Be Specific:** Details make your letter more personal and touching. Mention specific moments and qualities.
- **Use Scripture:** If you feel moved, include a Bible verse that reflects your feelings or serves as a prayer for your spouse.
- **Embrace Imperfection:** It is okay to feel vulnerable or unsure. Sharing those feelings can strengthen your bond.

Day 39: True Intimacy

Whoever would foster love covers over an offense,
but whoever repeats the matter separates close friends.

Proverbs 17:9

Today, let us reflect on the depth of intimacy beyond physical connections, focusing on the emotional, intellectual, and spiritual union that God intends for marriage. True intimacy mirrors Christ's relationship with us - it is about knowing and being known, in all aspects of our being. This divine connection is not just about sharing joys but also about understanding and sharing in each other's sorrows, fears, and dreams. It requires empathy, open communication, and a commitment to grow together spiritually. As we strive to deepen our marital bonds, let us remember that intimacy is an act of worship, honoring God's design for a unified, loving partnership that reflects His love for us. Let's commit to fostering this holistic intimacy, recognizing and responding to our spouse's needs, and nurturing a connection that transcends the physical, embracing the emotional and spiritual closeness God desires for us.

📖 Daily Prayer

Heavenly Father,

Thank You for the gift of marriage and the opportunity it presents to know and be known in a manner that reflects Your love for us. Help us to understand and cherish the true depth of intimacy You designed for our relationships. Teach us to communicate openly, to listen empathetically, and to support each other in every aspect of life. Guide us in recognizing and responding to each other's bids for affection, ensuring that no part of our shared life goes unnoticed or unvalued. Strengthen our bond, Lord, and fill our marriage with Your grace, patience, and love. May our relationship honor You and be a testament to the divine love that binds us together.

In Jesus' name, Amen.

📖 Read: Chapter 12, Pages 278-283

In "Beyond the Surface" we explore the concept of intimacy in marriage beyond physical connections, emphasizing the importance of emotional, intellectual, and spiritual bonds as intended by God. This holistic approach to intimacy reflects Christ's relationship with the Church and is essential for a fulfilling and resilient marriage. True intimacy involves open communication, empathetic understanding, shared experiences, and spiritual unity, allowing couples to know and love each other fully. The text highlights the necessity of empathy and mutual understanding, urging couples to delve deeper into each other's emotions and experiences. It also addresses the challenges of navigating anger within a relationship, advocating for patience, active listening, and forgiveness, guided by biblical principles. By fostering this comprehensive form of intimacy, couples can strengthen their bond and reflect God's love in their union.

🔑 Key Points

- **Holistic Intimacy (Ephesians 5:31-32)**

  True intimacy encompasses more than just physical closeness; it involves connecting on emotional, intellectual, and spiritual levels, creating a multi-dimensional bond that reflects the comprehensive love Christ has for the Church. This depth of connection ensures that both partners feel fully understood, valued, and connected, not just physically but in every aspect of their shared life.

- **Empathy and Understanding (1 Peter 3:7)**

  Empathy in marriage means putting oneself in the other's shoes, truly understanding their feelings, and responding with compassion and support. This deep level of understanding fosters a safe and nurturing environment where both partners feel seen, heard, and loved, paving the way for a more resilient and fulfilling relationship.

- **Communication and Shared Experiences (James 1:19)**

  Effective communication and the creation of shared experiences are the bedrock of lasting intimacy. By openly sharing thoughts, dreams, and fears, and by making memories together, couples can strengthen their bond and ensure that their relationship continues to grow and evolve over time.

- **Navigating Anger (Ephesians 4:26-27)**

  Constructively dealing with anger involves recognizing the emotion without letting it lead to sin, understanding its root causes, and addressing it with patience and love. This approach prevents resentment from building and allows couples to resolve conflicts in a way that strengthens their relationship rather than weakening it.

- **Spiritual Unity (Ecclesiastes 4:12)**

    Sharing a spiritual bond and aligning the marriage with biblical principles provide a strong foundation for intimacy. This unity in faith and purpose guides couples through life's ups and downs, enriches their relationship with deeper meaning, and aligns their journey with God's plan, fostering a profound sense of togetherness and mutual support.

Personal Reflection

Think about how you show and experience intimacy in your marriage. Does it go beyond the physical to include emotional, intellectual, and spiritual connection? Consider one way you can deepen your intimacy to strengthen your relationship in all areas.

_____
_____
_____
_____
_____
_____
_____
_____
_____
_____

Couple's Discussion

Consider together the role of empathy in your marriage. Share moments when you felt truly understood by your spouse and times when you felt disconnected. Confess any struggles with impatience, distraction, or misunderstanding that may have hindered empathy. Discuss how you can intentionally cultivate a deeper, more compassionate connection, modeling Christ's love and understanding in your daily interactions.

Harmony In Marriage: Couple's Workbook

Day 40: The Battle Within

Do not be anxious about anything, but in every situation, by prayer and petition, with thanksgiving, present your requests to God. ⁷ *And the peace of God, which transcends all understanding, will guard your hearts and your minds in Christ Jesus.*

Philippians 4:6-7

In the sacred journey of marriage, we go through various seasons, some of which are filled with joy, and others present challenges such as fear and anxiety. Although these emotions are natural, they can create barriers between spouses and God. However, Scripture offers us a divine solution: prayer and surrender. We invite His peace into our lives and relationships by bringing our worries and fears before God with a grateful heart. This peace is a divine gift that transcends our human understanding and can protect our hearts and minds, anchoring our marriages in Christ's love and security. As we navigate the complexities of life together, let us remember to rely on God's unfailing love and guidance and not on our own understanding.

📖 Daily Prayer

Heavenly Father,

We come before You today, bringing all our fears, anxieties, and worries that burden our hearts. In our marriage, help us to support each other with empathy, understanding, and love, just as You love us. Teach us to cast all our anxieties on You, knowing that You care deeply for us. Fill our hearts with Your peace that transcends understanding, guarding our minds and hearts in Christ Jesus. Help us to communicate openly, to listen with empathy, and to support each other in every challenge we face. May our marriage be a testament to Your love and faithfulness.

In Jesus' name, Amen.

📖 Read: Chapter 12, Pages 284-291

Today's reding emphasizes the importance of addressing fear, anxiety, depression, and grief within the sanctity of marriage through a biblical lens, advocating for empathy, understanding, and spiritual support between spouses. It underscores the necessity of prayer, mutual vulnerability, and reliance on God to navigate these challenges, reinforcing the idea that marriage should be a reflection of Christ's love and a journey of shared spiritual growth. The guidance provided aims to transform individual struggles into collective strengths, deepening the marital bond and fostering a more profound intimacy that transcends mere physical connection.

🔑 Key Points

- **Addressing Emotional Challenges Together (Ecclesiastes 4:9-10)**

    In facing emotional challenges such as fear, anxiety, depression, and grief, it is crucial for spouses to act as each other's support system, offering a listening ear, a shoulder to lean on, and a hand to hold. This collective approach not only alleviates the weight of such burdens but also reinforces the unity and strength of the marital bond, making the couple more resilient against life's adversities.

- **Prayer and Spiritual Support (Matthew 18:19-20)**

    Engaging in prayer and seeking God's guidance together provides a powerful foundation for overcoming emotional and mental struggles within the marriage. This spiritual practice invites divine intervention and fosters a sense of peace and clarity, enabling couples to navigate their challenges with a faith-centered perspective and a deeper sense of purpose.

- **Creating a Safe Space for Vulnerability (James 5:16)**

    Establishing an environment of trust and safety where both partners feel comfortable expressing their deepest fears and vulnerabilities is essential for emotional intimacy. This safe space encourages open communication and mutual understanding, which are fundamental for healing, growth, and the strengthening of the marital relationship.

- **Understanding and Patience (Colossians 3:12-13)**

    Taking the time to truly understand the root causes of a partner's emotional state—be it past traumas, current stressors, or future anxieties—requires patience and a non-judgmental attitude. This empathetic approach allows for effective support and reassurance, helping the afflicted spouse feel seen, heard, and valued, which is instrumental in the healing process.

- **Reconnecting with Christ (James 4:8)**

    By recentering the marriage around Christ and His teachings, couples can rediscover the spiritual and emotional intimacy that may have been lost. This reconnection with faith can guide spouses towards forgiveness, renewed love, and a stronger, more committed partnership. Embracing Christ's example of unconditional love and compassion can transform individual and shared struggles into opportunities for spiritual growth and deeper connection.

✒ Personal Reflection

Think about your spiritual practices as a couple. How often do you share your fears and anxieties and turn them over to God in prayer together? Consider one way to strengthen your spiritual connection, drawing from Proverbs 9:10, 'The fear of the Lord is the beginning of wisdom.'

_____
_____
_____
_____
_____
_____
_____
_____

💍 Couple's Discussion

Talk about a recent time when one or both of you felt overwhelmed by fear or anxiety. How did it impact your communication and emotional connection? Confess any struggles with withdrawing, reacting, or carrying burdens alone. Share how you felt during this time and discuss how you can support each other with mutual vulnerability, strength, and faith. Consider creating a new routine—such as nightly prayer or quiet reflection—to bring peace and unity to your marriage in difficult moments.

Day 41: Unrelenting Compassion

But Ruth replied, "Don't urge me to leave you or to turn back from you. Where you go I will go, and where you stay I will stay. Your people will be my people and your God my God.

Ruth 1:16

In marriage, understanding and compassion are key elements that strengthen the bond between spouses. The story of Ruth and Naomi from the Book of Ruth offers a profound example of empathy and commitment that extends beyond traditional marital relationships, illustrating the depth of bond that can exist when we truly care for one another. Ruth's famous declaration, "Where you go, I will go, and where you stay, I will stay. Your people will be my people and your God my God" (Ruth 1:16), embodies the essence of empathy and commitment.

This narrative invites us to consider the depth of our commitment and understanding towards our spouse. Are we willing to stand by them in times of uncertainty and change? Do we strive to understand their perspective and share in their journey, regardless of the challenges that may arise? Despite her grief and uncertainty, Ruth's loyalty to Naomi is a powerful example of the selfless love and empathy that should be mirrored in our marriages.

Let the story of Ruth inspire you to foster a deeper connection with your spouse. Reflect on how you can be more present and supportive, committing to walk beside them through all of life's seasons. Embrace the opportunity to deepen your emotional bond, turning every challenge into a chance to demonstrate your commitment and empathy, much like Ruth did for Naomi.

📖 Daily Prayer

Heavenly Father,

We come as partners in marriage, seeking to reflect the loyalty, love, and understanding of Ruth and Naomi. Teach us to listen with open hearts, share burdens with compassion, and stand by each other in all seasons. May our union reflect Your grace and faithfulness, and may our home be a sanctuary of Your presence

In Your holy name, we pray,

Amen.

📖 Read: Chapter 12, Pages 291-299

Building emotional connections in a marriage is about the small, consistent efforts that deepen bonds between partners. Active listening, spending quality time together, expressing physical affection, sharing vulnerabilities, and practicing empathy are key to fostering a closer relationship. Regularly expressing appreciation and gratitude, engaging in meaningful communication, setting shared goals, maintaining a spiritual connection through prayer, and creating intimate moments beyond the physical are all crucial. These actions help to build a foundation of trust, understanding, and mutual respect, transforming everyday interactions into opportunities for strengthening the marital bond.

🔑 Key Points

- **Active Listening (Luke 8:18)**

    Truly listening to your partner involves more than just hearing their words; it requires engagement and responsiveness. By providing undivided attention and responding thoughtfully, you validate your partner's feelings and contribute to a safer, more open relationship environment.

- **Quality Time (Psalm 63:1)**

    Quality time is not just about being in the same room but about being mentally and emotionally present. This dedicated time, free from distractions like phones or television, allows couples to explore new activities, engage in meaningful conversations, and reinforce their bond.

- **Physical Affection (Song of Solomon 2:6)**

    Touch is a powerful communicator of love and belonging. Simple gestures like a warm hug, a gentle kiss, or a reassuring hand squeeze can significantly boost feelings of security and attachment between partners, making the relationship more resilient.

- **Vulnerability and Empathy (Isaiah 53:4)**

    Being vulnerable means opening up about your innermost thoughts, fears, and desires without fear of judgment. When both partners can share openly and receive each other's truths with empathy, it creates a deeper level of intimacy and mutual respect that is essential for a strong, enduring relationship.

- **Appreciation and Communication (1 Thessalonians 5:11)**

    Regularly expressing appreciation for even the smallest acts can make your partner feel valued and loved. Effective communication involves not only talking about your needs and concerns but also listening and responding to your partner's. This reciprocal exchange nurtures a healthy, supportive relationship dynamic.

🪶 Personal Reflection

Consider a recent interaction where you practiced active listening with your spouse. How did you show genuine interest in their thoughts and feelings? What did this moment teach you about them or your relationship?

_____
_____
_____
_____
_____

💍 Couple's Discussion

Discuss how you can incorporate more intentional quality time into your daily routines, not just during date nights or special occasions. Explore small, meaningful ways to deepen your emotional connection and strengthen your bond, even amidst life's busyness.

Day 42: Tapestry of Grace

Above all, love each other deeply, because love covers over a multitude of sins.

1 Peter 4:8

In a world full of distractions, emotional fidelity shines as a cornerstone of marriage. It reflects the strength found in vulnerability, the beauty of shared empathy, and the power of unconditional love. Emotional fidelity creates a sanctuary in marriage—a safe space to share fears, dreams, and imperfections, knowing they will be met with acceptance and understanding.

When we open our hearts, love deepens, trust grows, and Christ knits our souls together in grace and forgiveness. This connection allows couples to weather life's storms with unity and strength.

Take time to reflect: How has vulnerability deepened your bond? How has empathy helped you see the world through your spouse's eyes? Let Christ's love guide you as you make emotional fidelity a pillar of your marriage, building a relationship grounded in trust and grace.

Daily Prayer

Heavenly Father,

Thank You for guiding us through a week of exploring the depths of emotional fidelity in our marriage. Please help us continue fostering an environment of empathy, understanding, and vulnerability. Teach us to love deeply, forgive freely, and support each other unconditionally, mirroring Your love for us. May our marriage reflect Your grace, a testament to the power of Your love, and a sanctuary of emotional fidelity.

Amen.

Personal Reflection

Recall a moment when vulnerability with your spouse was difficult. What obstacles did you face, and how can you address these challenges to strengthen emotional fidelity in your marriage?

_____
_____
_____
_____
_____
_____

⚭ Couple's Discussion

Reflect on the concepts of intimacy and vulnerability from this week. Share a moment when being vulnerable created a strong sense of intimacy in your relationship. What fears or hesitations did you face, and how did overcoming them strengthen your connection? Discuss practical steps you can take together to create a safe space for vulnerability, deepening your emotional fidelity and connection.

WEEK SEVEN: SEXUAL FIDELITY

Day 43: Sexual Fidelity

Love is patient, love is kind. It does not envy, it does not boast, it is not proud. ⁵ It does not dishonor others, it is not self-seeking, it is not easily angered, it keeps no record of wrongs.

1 Corinthians 13:4-5

In a world where the meanings and boundaries of sexuality are constantly debated and redefined, it is crucial to return to the foundational truths laid out in Scripture. The text underlines a profound truth that sexual fidelity is not just about the physical act of being with one's spouse but encompasses mental and emotional faithfulness as well. This teaching echoes Jesus' words, emphasizing that even a lustful look can betray the covenant of marriage.

Sexual fidelity is a multifaceted commitment that reflects God's unwavering love and loyalty to us. It is about creating a sacred space within the marriage where trust, emotional intimacy, and spiritual unity can flourish. This unity is not just for the couple's benefit but serves as a testament to God's covenantal love for humanity.

In the act of sexual fidelity, we find a divine command and a blessing. It is a practice of mutual respect and love that mirrors Christ's love for the church—a love so deep that He gave His life for it. The marital bond, fortified by fidelity, becomes a living metaphor for divine love and a sanctuary for God's presence in the couple's life.

📖 Daily Prayer

Heavenly Father,

Thank You for the gift of marriage and the union it represents. Help us honor You through sexual fidelity, reflecting Your steadfast love. Guide us to nurture our relationship with purity and faithfulness, cherishing and respecting one another as Your gift. Strengthen our bond to overcome challenges and grow in love, making our marriage a testament to Your grace.

In Jesus' name, we pray,
Amen.

📖 Read: Chapter 13, Pages 300-304

This chapter addresses the complex issue of sexual fidelity within marriage, emphasizing that it encompasses more than just avoiding adultery but includes mental and emotional loyalty as well. It discusses the idolatry of sex in contemporary society and contrasts it with the biblical understanding of sex as a profound expression of unity, intimacy, and a reflection of God's character within the covenant of marriage. The text underlines the importance of sexual exclusivity in fostering trust, deepening emotional intimacy, and strengthening the marital bond, which, in turn, aligns the marriage with divine purposes and serves as an act of worship and obedience to God.

🔑 Key Points

- **Cultural Idolatry vs. Biblical View of Sexuality (1 John 2:16)**
  The text contrasts the modern idolization of sex and sexual identity with the biblical view, where sexual fidelity is a marker of a healthy relationship, deeply integrated with love, purity, and faithfulness. This idolatry, pervasive in media, education, and politics, distorts the true beauty and purpose of sex, which is designed to be celebrated within the bounds of marriage.

- **Sexual Fidelity Beyond Physical Acts (Matthew 5:28)**
  Sexual fidelity in a biblical marriage extends beyond avoiding physical adultery, encompassing mental and emotional loyalty. This comprehensive view is in line with Jesus' teaching that even lustful thoughts can breach marital faithfulness, pointing towards a deeper understanding of fidelity that reflects God's unwavering love for His people.

- **The Significance of Sexual Exclusivity (Hebrews 13:4)**
  Within marriage, sexual exclusivity is crucial for building trust, emotional intimacy, and a strong partnership. It acts as a continual reaffirmation of marriage vows and nurtures the marital bond, thereby embodying God's covenantal love and deepening the couple's relationship with Him.

- **Sex as a Divine Expression and Covenant (Genesis 2:24, Ephesians 5:31-32)**
  Sex is depicted as a divine expression of unity and intimacy, reflecting God's creative power and character. It is not only for procreation or pleasure but serves as a testament to unity, mirroring the lifelong commitment to love and honor one another, akin to Christ's love for the Church. The marital act of sex becomes a spiritual act of worship, celebrating the sacred institution of marriage.

- **Biological and Spiritual Significance of Sexual Union (1 Corinthians 6:19-20)**

The chapter highlights how the biological aspects of sexual intimacy, like the release of oxytocin, align with scriptural principles, fostering a deep connection that mirrors God's design for marriage. This union is not solely physical but also spiritual, serving as an outward expression of the soul and emphasizing the importance of sexual fidelity for the health and sanctity of marriage.

Personal Reflection

Reflect on how sexual fidelity is lived out in your thoughts and emotions, not just your actions. Are there ways you could grow in being fully present and loyal to your spouse? Think about how building trust and emotional intimacy through exclusivity strengthens your connection and consider steps to protect this part of your relationship.

_____
_____
_____
_____
_____
_____
_____
_____
_____
_____
_____

Couple's Discussion

Discuss the concept of 'one flesh' in marriage, encompassing physical, spiritual, and emotional union in love and mutual submission. Reflect on how viewing sexual intimacy as a testament to unity, grace, and God's covenant shapes your understanding of this gift. Share ways you can honor this perspective in your marriage by fostering mutual discovery, joy, and a deeper connection with each other and with God.

Day 44: A Renewed Heart

If we confess our sins, he is faithful and just and will forgive us our sins and purify us from all unrighteousness.

1 John 1:9

Sexual infidelity deeply damages the trust that marriage is built on, leaving pain and betrayal in its wake. Yet, even in such brokenness, God's grace offers hope for forgiveness and restoration. Through sincere repentance and a willingness to forgive, healing becomes possible, reflecting God's redemptive power.

In today's world, where sexual fidelity is often blurred, protecting the sanctity of marriage requires intentional effort. Challenges like pornography, social media, and cultural pressures can strain relationships, but Christ's promise of healing remains steadfast.

True restoration goes beyond addressing infidelity itself; it involves reconnecting emotionally and spiritually. Healing comes through reestablishing trust, understanding past wounds, and rebuilding intimacy grounded in God's design for love and respect. Let God's grace guide you toward unity and renewal, showing His power to mend even the deepest hurts.

📖 Daily Prayer

Heavenly Father,

We come to You seeking protection over our hearts and our marriage. Guard us from temptation and anything that could harm our trust and unity. Strengthen our bond and help us remain faithful to each other in thought, word, and action.

If betrayal has touched our relationship, we ask for Your grace to forgive and heal. Protect us from bitterness and resentment, and guide us toward reconciliation and renewed trust. Help us to reflect Your love, offering forgiveness as You have forgiven us.

Surround our marriage with Your peace and shield it from the pressures of this world. May Your presence be a constant reminder of the commitment we have made to You and to each other. Lead us to walk together in love, grace, and unity, trusting in Your power to protect and restore.

Amen.

📖 Read: Chapter 13, Pages 304-308

The reading for today discusses the profound impact of sexual infidelity on marriage, highlighting how it breaches trust, causes deep emotional wounds, and creates a spiritual divide between partners and God. It emphasizes the contradiction of infidelity with biblical teachings on marriage, transforming an act meant to honor God into one of deceit. Despite the devastation, the text offers hope through God's grace, which enables forgiveness, healing, and restoration. The current societal landscape, characterized by blurred lines around sexual fidelity and the normalization of behaviors that undermine marital sanctity, adds complexity to maintaining sexual purity. The text identifies various forms of infidelity, including pornography, emotional affairs, and secretive behaviors, each contributing to the erosion of trust and intimacy. It advocates for addressing the deeper emotional and spiritual issues underlying infidelity, emphasizing the possibility of healing and renewed commitment through God's transformative power.

🔑 Key Points

- **Devastating Impact of Infidelity (Proverbs 6:32-33)**

  Sexual infidelity severely damages marriages, leading to emotional distress, a breach of trust, and a spiritual disconnect from God. The act contradicts biblical values, turning what should be a God-glorifying relationship into one marred by deceit and betrayal.

- **Healing Through God's Grace (Psalm 51:10-12)**

  Despite the deep scars left by infidelity, there is a path to recovery through God's grace. This journey involves repentance from the offending partner, forgiveness from the betrayed, and a mutual dedication to healing. God's promise to forgive and purify us offers hope for restoring trust and intimacy in the marriage.

- **Challenges in Contemporary Culture (Romans 12:2)**

  Today's society complicates the biblical understanding of sexual fidelity. The widespread acceptance of behaviors like pornography, extramarital affairs facilitated by technology, and a culture that prizes self-expression over covenantal fidelity challenge couples to maintain sexual purity within their marriages.

- **Broad Definition of Infidelity (Matthew 5:28)**

  The text outlines a comprehensive view of infidelity, including not only physical adultery but also pornography, emotional affairs, and any behavior that violates the sanctity of the marriage covenant. These actions undermine the trust, unity, and mutual respect foundational to a healthy marriage.

- **Addressing Underlying Issues for True Healing (James 5:16)**
  Healing from infidelity requires more than just overcoming the immediate betrayal; it involves addressing the deeper emotional and spiritual disconnections within the marriage. This process demands honesty, vulnerability, and a reliance on God's strength to rebuild a marriage that reflects His design for intimacy, fidelity, and love.

Personal Reflection

Recall a time when forgiveness was essential in healing from betrayal or hurt. How did offering or receiving forgiveness change your perspective on vulnerability and trust? Reflect on how God's grace influenced this process and identify one step to cultivate forgiveness in your relationships.

_____
_____
_____
_____
_____
_____
_____
_____

Couple's Discussion

Discuss the external pressures and cultural influences, such as pornography, social media, and societal views on sexuality, that challenge sexual fidelity in marriage. Share openly about any struggles or fears these influences may have caused. Together, commit to transparency, accountability, and mutual support. Identify practical steps to protect the sanctity of your marriage and deepen your physical and emotional intimacy in a way that reflects God's design and honors each other.

Day 45: Looking Forward

God is our refuge and strength,
an ever-present help in trouble.

Psalm 46:1

In the depths of our brokenness, especially in the wake of sexual infidelity, we find ourselves standing at the crossroads of pain and forgiveness, shame and grace. The revelation of infidelity not only shatters trust but also embeds a deep sense of betrayal in the heart, making the path to healing seem insurmountable. Yet, in these very shadows of our lives, the light of God's grace shines the brightest, offering hope, healing, and a way forward.

The journey of healing from infidelity is complex and layered. It demands an honest confrontation with the pain, an understanding of the underlying issues that led to the betrayal, and a heartfelt commitment to rebuild the brokenness. This process is not about forgetting the hurt but about transforming it, allowing God's grace to mend the fractures and create something new and stronger from the pieces.

Sexual infidelity, while a betrayal of the vows made before God, opens a door to understanding the profound depth of forgiveness and redemption that Christ offers. Just as Jesus expanded the definition of adultery to include the desires of the heart, He also broadened the scope of grace, offering forgiveness and restoration to all who seek it with a contrite heart.

In the narrative of Anna and Caleb, we see a vivid illustration of the pain caused by infidelity but also the potential for redemption. Their story is a testament to the power of God's grace to heal the deepest wounds and restore trust and intimacy in a marriage. It is a reminder that, even in the midst of betrayal, God's love remains steadfast, calling us to a journey of healing that is grounded in forgiveness, understanding, and renewed commitment.

📖 Daily Prayer

Heavenly Father,

Lord, in our pain and betrayal, we turn to You, our refuge and strength. Help us confront the brokenness, extend forgiveness as You have forgiven us, and rebuild trust and intimacy in our marriages. May Your grace guide us from shame to healing and restoration.

In Jesus' Name,

Amen.

📖 Read: Chapter 13, Pages 308-314

🔑 Key Points

- **The Multifaceted Nature of Infidelity (Ephesians 4:31-32)**

    Infidelity extends beyond physical betrayal, rooted in a complex web of emotional disconnection, loneliness, and personal trauma. This perspective urges individuals to look beyond surface-level actions and consider the profound emotional and spiritual rifts that infidelity can create in a marriage.

- **Cultural Versus Biblical Understanding of Infidelity (Job 31:1-4)**

    The text contrasts the salacious, superficial treatment of sexual infidelity in culture with a biblical approach that sees it as a violation of a divine covenant. This dichotomy highlights the importance of approaching infidelity with grace and understanding, focusing on the covenantal aspect of marriage as outlined in scriptures like Matthew 5:28.

- **Healing and Restoration Through God (1 Peter 5:10)**

    Emphasizing the transformative power of God's grace, the narrative offers hope for marriages shattered by infidelity. It underscores the need for sincere repentance, forgiveness, and the rebuilding of trust and intimacy through a shared commitment to a God-centered relationship.

- **Confronting Underlying Issues with Honesty and Courage (James 5:16)**

    Addressing infidelity involves delving into the underlying personal and relational issues. This process is crucial for healing, as it moves beyond merely treating symptoms to addressing the root causes of betrayal, thereby fostering deeper understanding and empathy within the marriage.

- **The Role of Community and Faith in Recovery (Galatians 6:2)**

    The journey from betrayal to restoration is not meant to be walked alone. The support of a faith-based community, coupled with the guiding principles of scripture, plays a pivotal role in guiding couples through the challenges of reconciliation, highlighting the importance of surrounding oneself with a network of support that aligns with biblical values of forgiveness and restoration.

🪶 Personal Reflection

Reflect on how past traumas, fears, or cultural influences have shaped your understanding of intimacy and fidelity. Confess how these have negatively impacted your relationship, and consider how addressing these issues with God's help could deepen your connection with your spouse and Him.

_____
_____
_____
_____
_____
_____
_____
_____

💍 Couple's Discussion

Discuss how you can turn to God together for healing, forgiveness, and strength in rebuilding your marital bond on true intimacy, vulnerability, and faith. Confess any fears, frustrations, or wounds that have contributed to emotional or spiritual disconnection. Explore ways to support each other in addressing these underlying issues, and consider how your journey toward healing can deepen both your connection with each other and your relationship with God.

Day 46: Song of Love

Let him kiss me with the kisses of his mouth—
for your love is more delightful than wine.

Song of Songs 1:2

In the Song of Solomon, we are invited into a garden of love and intimacy, where the language of love is both sacred and profoundly human. This verse opens a poetic discourse on the beauty and intensity of love, setting a tone of deep affection and mutual delight. It reminds us that the expression of love within marriage is a gift, a treasure that reflects both human and divine passion.

The love described in Song of Solomon is rich with desire, respect, and admiration. It portrays a relationship where both partners are fully engaged in expressing their love for one another. This book challenges us to view our intimate relationships through a lens of sacredness and joy, recognizing the unique way marital love mirrors God's love for us.

We must strive to cultivate this depth of affection and appreciation in our marriages. May we see our partners with eyes full of love and grace, eager to express our affection in ways that honor them and reflect the beauty of our Creator's design for love. As we navigate the complexities of life together, let the poetry of Solomon remind us to pause and revel in the simple, profound joy of loving and being loved.

📖 Daily Prayer

Dear Lord,

Thank You for the gift of love and the joy of marital intimacy. Help us to cherish and honor our spouse in a way that reflects Your love for us. May our relationship be filled with the delight and affection described in the Song of Solomon. Teach us to communicate our love both in words and in actions, always seeking to deepen our bond and understanding of each other.

Amen.

👫 Fidelity Builder: Song of Solomon

This activity is designed to foster deeper understanding and appreciation for intimacy in marriage through the poetic and intimate lens of the Song of Solomon. By engaging with this beautiful Biblical text, couples can explore love, desire, and fidelity themes in a safe and spiritual context. This fidelity builder is an invitation to explore the sacredness of marital intimacy through Scripture, strengthening your bond and commitment to each other in the process.

Preparation

- Each of you should have access to a Bible or a digital version of the Song of Solomon (Song of Songs in some translations).
- Create a comfortable and private space where you both can discuss without interruptions.

Instructions:

1. **Reading Together**

   Set aside a specific time to read the Song of Solomon together. You might choose to read aloud to one another or silently and then share your thoughts.

2. **Reflection**

   After reading, take some time to reflect on the imagery, language, and emotions conveyed in the passages. Consider what these verses reveal about God's design for marital love and intimacy.

3. **Discussion Prompts**
   - How do the expressions of love and desire in the Song of Solomon reflect our own experiences of intimacy?
   - In what ways does this book affirm the beauty and importance of sexual fidelity and physical connection in marriage?
   - How can we incorporate the appreciation of each other's beauty and worth, as exemplified in the Song of Solomon, into our daily lives?

4. **Creative Expression**

   Inspired by the poetic nature of the Song of Solomon, each of you should writes a short love note, poem, or letter to the other, expressing admiration, desire, and commitment. Emphasize qualities you cherish and affirm your dedication to nurturing intimacy in your relationship.

5. **Exchange and Discuss**

Share your written expressions with each other. Take this opportunity to openly communicate about your feelings, desires, and any areas you wish to grow in together.

6. **Prayer**

As always, conclude your activity with a prayer, asking God to bless your marriage with the depth of love, joy, and intimacy depicted in the Song of Solomon. Pray for guidance in building a marriage that reflects His love and fidelity.

Notes for Couples

- Approach this activity with openness, sensitivity, and respect for each other's feelings and boundaries.
- Remember, the goal is to deepen your connection and understanding of God's vision for marital intimacy, not to create discomfort or pressure.
- This activity can be revisited periodically to continually enrich and reaffirm the intimate bond between you.

Harmony In Marriage: Couple's Workbook

Day 47: Healing Together

Restore to me the joy of your salvation
and grant me a willing spirit, to sustain me.

Psalm 51:12

The journey of healing from infidelity is marked by a path of repentance, a deep, transformative process that goes beyond mere acknowledgment of wrongdoing. Psalm 51:12 expresses a heartfelt plea for the restoration of joy and the sustenance of a willing spirit, highlighting the essential role of divine intervention in the healing process. Genuine repentance involves a complete turning away from sinful behaviors, guided by a contrite heart that seeks not only the forgiveness of the offended partner but also the mercy of God. This process is not a solitary journey but one that is supported by the community of believers, biblical counseling, and the unshakeable hope found in Christ's promise of renewal. As individuals and couples navigate the tumultuous waters of betrayal, they are called to anchor themselves in the steadfast love and forgiveness of God, allowing His grace to guide them towards a future defined by honesty, trust, and a deeper, more abiding love.

📖 Daily Prayer

Heavenly Father,

In our brokenness, we seek Your healing and restoration. We confess the pain caused by infidelity and turn to You with contrite hearts. Grant us grace to rebuild trust, forgive, and find strength in Your promises. May our journey reflect Your redemptive love and glorify Your name.

In Jesus' Name, we pray,

Amen.

📖 Read: Chapter 13, Pages 314-318

Today's reading explores a profound journey of healing from infidelity within a marriage, emphasizing that through Christ, restoration is not only possible but also deeply transformative. It calls for genuine repentance from the unfaithful partner, involving a heartfelt turnaround and commitment to forsaking past behaviors, underscored by Psalm 51:17's call for a contrite heart. The betrayed spouse is equally tasked with the challenge of forgiveness, a process facilitated by scriptural exhortations like Ephesians 4:31-32 and supported by the community of believers, as described in Galatians 6:2. Hope, anchored in scriptures like Hebrews 6:19, serves as a crucial element in navigating the emotional turmoil post-infidelity, with biblical counseling playing a pivotal role in addressing underlying issues and guiding couples towards a renewed future. The narrative asserts that through dedicated effort, transparent communication, and divine grace, marriages can emerge from the trial of infidelity strengthened, purified, and more deeply rooted in Christ's redemptive love.

🗝 Key Points

- **Genuine Repentance and Transformation (Psalm 51:17)**

    Healing from infidelity begins with sincere repentance, which is more than acknowledging wrongdoing; it is a transformative journey that requires abandoning sinful behaviors, guided by a heart that seeks forgiveness not only from the spouse but also from God, aligning with the essence of Psalm 51:17.

- **Forgiveness as a Path to Liberation (Ephesians 4:31-32)**

    The process of forgiveness for the betrayed partner is challenging but essential for personal and relational healing. It is an act of will, supported by faith and community, that frees the individual from resentment and bitterness, reflecting the forgiveness Christ offers us, as emphasized in Ephesians 4:31-32.

- **The Role of Hope and Community in Healing (Hebrews 6:19, Galatians 6:2)**

    Hope, described as an anchor in Hebrews 6:19, plays a vital role in overcoming the emotional aftermath of betrayal. The support and accountability from a faith-based community, as advocated in Galatians 6:2, are indispensable in navigating the complexities of reconciliation and restoration.

- **Biblical Counseling for Deeper Understanding (Psalm 51:10-12)**

    Addressing the root causes of infidelity and fostering mutual understanding are critical steps in the healing process, achievable through biblical counseling. This approach equips couples with communication tools, helps them to rebuild trust, and encourages a deeper exploration of emotional and spiritual needs.

- **Renewal Through Divine Strength (Philippians 4:13)**

    The journey of recovery from infidelity is marked by a steadfast focus on God's promises and a commitment to the hard work of healing. Couples must believe in the transformative power of the Holy

Spirit to sanctify their union, making it possible to start anew with honesty, trust, and a deeper, more abiding love, as they strive to reflect Christ's redemptive love in their relationship.

🪶 Personal Reflection

Think about the concept of genuine repentance. How do you move from acknowledging guilt to turning away from sinful behaviors? Confess areas where your heart may lack true contrition, and consider how embracing repentance can lead to healing and transformation.

_____
_____
_____
_____
_____
_____
_____
_____
_____
_____
_____

ⓘ Couple's Discussion

Discuss the importance of engaging with a community of believers as you heal from any form of infidelity, reflecting on Galatians 6:2. Confess any hesitations or struggles with openness and transparency in seeking support. Talk about how you can both actively seek and contribute to a community that aligns with biblical values, and consider how mutual support and accountability can help rebuild trust and strengthen your God-centered relationship.

Day 48: Fortifying Love

"For this reason a man will leave his father and mother and be united to his wife, and the two will become one flesh."[b] [32] *This is a profound mystery—but I am talking about Christ and the church.*

Ephesians 5:31-32

In marriage, intimacy goes beyond physical engagement. It is a profound spiritual and emotional connection that reflects the relationship between Christ and His Church. As believers, we must embrace this view of intimacy, where physical union is just one expression of a much larger covenantal love. This spiritual union is about giving and receiving in love, vulnerability, trust, and mutual submission, reflecting the essence of our relationship with God. As we deepen this holistic intimacy, our marriages become a testament to the power of God's design, transcending the temporary and reflecting something eternal. Let us commit to nurturing this depth of connection, celebrating the gift of marriage as a mirror of the divine. Every act of love and commitment echoes the unfathomable love Christ has for us.

📖 Daily Prayer

Dear Heavenly Father,

Thank You for the gift of marriage, a sacred covenant that reflects Your profound love for us. Help us to embrace the fullness of intimacy You desire for us, not just in physical union but in our spiritual and emotional connections as well. Teach us to love our spouse as Christ loves the Church, with selflessness, sacrifice, and unwavering commitment. May our relationship be a living testament to Your design, grounded in mutual respect, openness, and the joy of sharing life together. Strengthen us to guard our marriage against the challenges that may threaten its sanctity, and guide us in continually nurturing a bond that glorifies You in all aspects.

In Jesus' Name, Amen.

📖 Read: Chapter 13, Pages 318-326

"Building a Fortress of Intimacy and Trust" underscores the significance of sexual fidelity within the sacred confines of marriage, as instructed by biblical teachings. It highlights that true fidelity transcends mere physical exclusivity, weaving together emotional, spiritual, and physical connections to form a robust foundation for a godly union. The text encourages couples to engage in open communication, set boundaries to guard against temptations, and actively invest in their relationship beyond the physical aspect. It calls for a mutual submission and understanding that mirrors the devotion between Christ and the Church, emphasizing the creation of an exclusive, sacred space where intimacy and trust flourish, thereby reflecting the depth of commitment and love God intends for marriage.

🔑 Key Points

- **The Comprehensive Nature of Fidelity (1 Corinthians 13:4-7)**

    Sexual fidelity is presented not just as physical exclusivity but as an amalgamation of emotional, spiritual, and physical bonds. This holistic approach requires openness, honesty, and a commitment to building a deep connection, reflecting the multifaceted nature of a relationship designed by God.

- **The Role of Communication and Boundaries (James 1:19-20)**

    Effective communication about desires, expectations, and fears is paramount in cultivating a healthy sexual relationship within marriage. Additionally, setting clear boundaries to defend against external and internal temptations is crucial for maintaining the sanctity of the marital bond.

- **Investment Beyond Physical Intimacy (Ecclesiastes 4:9-12)**

    The importance of investing in the marital relationship beyond the bedroom is emphasized, suggesting acts of service, quality time, and spiritual activities as means to strengthen the bond. This investment enriches the emotional reservoir of both partners, enhancing the overall intimacy.

- **Mutual Submission and Respect (Ephesians 5:21-25)**

    The concept of mutual submission, comes from Ephesians 5:21, underscores the importance of valuing the needs and well-being of one's spouse. This principle fosters a servant-hearted love and respect, which are essential for a fulfilling sexual and emotional relationship.

- **Facing Challenges Together (Galatians 6:2)**

    The text acknowledges the threats of sexual infidelity, stemming from both physical desires and deeper emotional or spiritual issues. It advocates for a process of healing and restoration that involves repentance, genuine forgiveness, and a commitment to rebuilding trust, all within the framework of God's grace and guidance.

🪶 Personal Reflection

Reflect on the role of open communication in your marriage. Do you feel comfortable sharing your deepest desires and fears with your spouse? Confess any barriers to honesty and consider one step to strengthen transparency and trust in your relationship.

_____
_____
_____
_____
_____
_____
_____
_____

💍 Couple's Discussion

Discuss how you can invest in your relationship beyond physical intimacy by focusing on acts of service, quality time, spiritual activities, and other expressions of love. Confess any areas where you may have neglected these aspects of your connection. Explore how these intentional investments can strengthen your emotional and spiritual bond, enriching the overall intimacy in your marriage.

Day 49: A Healing Journey

He heals the brokenhearted
and binds up their wounds.

Psalm 147:3

As the chapter on sexual fidelity closes, couples are invited to reflect on the transformative journey they have traversed—a path that has illuminated the depth of their commitment, the necessity for mutual respect, and the healing power of Christ's unfailing love. Sexual fidelity, layered with complexities and vulnerabilities, can surface deep-seated pain and trauma. Yet, in the shadow of these challenges, Psalm 147:3 reminds us of God's tender care for the brokenhearted and His promise to mend the deepest wounds.

This period of reflection and healing is a sacred opportunity to surrender every hurt, misunderstanding, and moment of disconnect to the One who understands our pain more intimately than we might comprehend. It is a time to acknowledge that healing is not only possible but is actively offered by a God specializing in restoration and renewal. The journey toward healing is paved with grace, where every step taken is a step closer to experiencing the fullness of intimacy and love as God intended.

In the embrace of God's healing love, couples can find the strength to rebuild trust, to foster deeper connections, and to rediscover the joy of their union. This devotional serves as a reminder that in every moment of vulnerability, in every tear shed, and in every prayer whispered, God is there, gently binding up wounds and renewing spirits.

📖 Daily Prayer

Dear Lord,

In the quiet moments of reflection on our journey through the realms of sexual fidelity, we seek Your healing presence. You know every hurt we have experienced and every scar we carry. We ask for Your healing hands to be upon us, mending what has been broken and soothing what has been hurt. Help us to find strength in Your promises and comfort in Your love. Teach us to walk in forgiveness, to embrace healing, and to celebrate the gift of intimacy that You have blessed us with. May our relationship be a testament to Your restorative power and a reflection of Your unconditional love. In Jesus' Name,

Amen.

🪶 Personal Reflection

Think about your journey of understanding physical intimacy and sexual fidelity in light of this week's readings. How has your perspective shifted? Confess any areas needing growth, and consider how to nurture healing and progress in your marriage.

_____
_____
_____
_____
_____
_____
_____
_____
_____
_____
_____

💍 Couple's Discussion

As you reflect on this week's focus on sexual fidelity and physical intimacy, share the discoveries or challenges that impacted you most. Talk about how you can work together to address areas of trauma, healing, or growth to strengthen your bond and honor God in your marriage. Consider whether committing to biblical programs or seeking biblical counseling could support you in this journey.

WEEK EIGHT: SPIRITUAL FIDELITY

Day 50: Spiritual Fidelity

For our struggle is not against flesh and blood, but against the rulers, against the authorities, against the powers of this dark world and against the spiritual forces of evil in the heavenly realms.

Ephesians 6:12

Scripture provides direct and deep understanding into the real nature of our conflicts, not solely as individuals but also, and more critically within our marriages and families. The Word informs us that our encounters, particularly those affecting our spiritual loyalty, are rooted in a spiritual conflict that transcends physical adversaries. This understanding urges us to adopt a perspective of spiritual readiness within our marriage, employing prayer, sacred texts, and shared faith as our tools of defense.

Navigating the marital voyage involves traversing both joyful peaks and challenging valleys, with each spouse sharing in the other's burdens and triumphs, as well as their spiritual development. When both partners recognize and embrace the spiritual essence of their relationship, they are better equipped to fortify themselves with faith, hope, and love. These virtues are crucial for facing and overcoming the various challenges life and unseen spiritual adversaries may present, aiming to weaken their connection.

Daily Prayer

Heavenly Father,

We come united in marriage, knowing our struggles are not just physical but also spiritual. Protect and guide us, clothing us in Your armor to stand firm against the enemy. Strengthen our faith and bond, making our marriage a testament to Your power and love. May we grow closer to each other and deeper in You.

In Jesus' Name, we pray, Amen.

📖 Read: Chapter 14, Pages 327-333

Spiritual fidelity within a biblical marriage encompasses a deep, mutual dedication between partners to foster and maintain their faith in God together, through shared beliefs, prayer, worship, and scriptural study. This foundational element acts as the support for all other dimensions of marital unity, including emotional, intellectual, and physical bonds. The principles derived from key scriptural passages guide how spouses interact with love, respect, and consideration for each other, fostering a cycle of growth that brings them closer to each other and to God. This journey is not without its challenges; lapses in spiritual fidelity, through actions that undermine the spiritual bond or disregard the partner's spiritual journey, can significantly strain the marriage. However, the path to healing and strengthening this bond lies in mutual support, understanding, and a commitment to navigating life's hurdles with faith at the forefront.

🔑 Key Points

- **Mutual Spiritual Commitment (Ecclesiastes 4:12, Proverbs 27:17)**
  The essence of spiritual fidelity in marriage is the shared commitment to living out one's faith together, engaging in practices like prayer and scripture study. This shared spiritual path is fundamental, acting as the core around which all other aspects of the relationship revolve, enhancing trust, intimacy, and mutual respect.

- **Challenges to Spiritual Unity (1 Peter 5:8)**
  Spiritual infidelity can manifest in various forms, including the neglect of shared spiritual practices, intellectualizing faith without heartfelt application, or prioritizing external religious activities over intimate spiritual growth. These actions can create significant rifts in the spiritual unity and overall harmony within the marriage.

- **Impact of Spiritual Harmony (Ephesians 5:31-32)**
  A strong spiritual connection within a marriage enriches the relationship, creating a resilient bond that is capable of withstanding life's challenges. It fosters a profound sense of oneness, mirroring the unity between Christ and the Church, and becomes a source of strength, comfort, and guidance for both partners.

- **Overcoming Spiritual Struggles (1 Thessalonians 5:4-11)**
  Addressing and healing from spiritual infidelity requires grace, forgiveness, and a willingness to rebuild trust. Couples must engage in open communication, seek mutual understanding, and recommit to shared spiritual growth, potentially with the support of biblical counseling.

- **Cultivating Spiritual Growth (Colossians 3:16)**

    To maintain and deepen spiritual fidelity, couples should engage in regular, joint spiritual activities that foster their connection to God and each other. This includes prayer, worship, and discussing spiritual matters openly and honestly, thus nurturing their spiritual bond and ensuring their marriage reflects their faith.

Personal Reflection

Reflect on how you contribute to the spiritual unity within your marriage. Are there moments when you might inadvertently contribute to spiritual discord, such as prioritizing personal desires over shared spiritual goals, or neglecting your partner's spiritual needs? Think about steps to address these challenges and enhance the spiritual bond between you and your spouse.

_____
_____
_____
_____
_____
_____
_____
_____
_____

Couple's Discussion

Explore your shared spiritual goals and reflect on the current state of your spiritual unity. Share the practices that have most strengthened your relationship with God and each other, and confess any areas where you've struggled to grow together. Discuss opportunities for spiritual growth you want to pursue as a couple, fostering a deeper understanding of each other's spiritual needs and how you can support one another in your faith journey.

Day 51: A Journey Back

But when you pray, go into your room, close the door and pray to your Father, who is unseen. Then your Father, who sees what is done in secret, will reward you.

Matthew 6:6

Amid life's busyness, it is easy for the spiritual connection between spouses to become just another item on an endless checklist, rather than the deep, binding force it is meant to be. Today, reflect on the spiritual altars within your marriage - those moments, routines, or practices where you both encounter God together. Consider the true depth of these interactions. Are they genuine meetings with the Divine that draw you closer to each other and to God, or have they slipped into mere formalities?

Contemplate the essence of your shared spiritual journey. It is not about the number of activities you do in the name of faith, but the quality of the spiritual intimacy you share. This sacred connection should be a source of unity, understanding, and mutual growth, deepening your commitment to one another as you both grow closer to God.

Let us aim to see our spiritual practices not as tasks to be checked off, but as opportunities to genuinely connect with our partner and with God. This simplified approach encourages us to cherish and prioritize our shared spiritual life, ensuring that our marriage reflects the profound love and fidelity that God desires for us.

📖 Daily Prayer

Heavenly Father,

We come before You to seek a deeper, more intimate connection with You and with each other. Help us to find peace and strength in the quiet places where Your voice is clear and Your presence is felt. Guide us to build our relationship on the foundation of shared faith and devotion, not just on outward expressions of spirituality. Teach us to prioritize our spiritual oneness, finding joy and fulfillment in the sacred moments we spend in Your presence together. Rekindle the flame of our spiritual intimacy, that our love for You and for each other may reflect the depth of Your love for us.

In Jesus' Name, we pray. Amen.

📖 Read: Chapter 14, Pages 333-337

Today's reading takes us with a couple deeply involved in church activities but experiencing a growing spiritual void in their private lives, the story highlights the importance of genuine spiritual intimacy over mere involvement in religious tasks. Despite their outward appearance of devout service, they confront the reality of their neglected personal spiritual connection, sparking a journey towards rekindling their shared faith as the core of their relationship. This testimony serves as a reminder of the pivotal role of spiritual fidelity in marriage, emphasizing it as the foundation upon which all other aspects of the relationship are built, influencing everything from emotional intimacy to mutual respect and shared purpose. It underlines the transformative power of a genuine spiritual bond, not just in navigating life's challenges but in deepening the marital connection.

🔑 Key Points

- **The Essence of Spiritual Intimacy (Genesis 2:24)**
  Genuine spiritual intimacy in a marriage goes beyond shared religious activities, forming the bedrock for a deep, meaningful connection. It is the quality of this spiritual bond that transforms routine tasks into profound interactions, nurturing the relationship and fostering a closer union with God.

- **Rekindling Spiritual Connection (Matthew 19:6)**
  The process of rekindling a spiritual connection requires a conscious effort to prioritize personal faith journeys within the marital context. This involves deliberate actions like shared prayer and Bible study, moving beyond the superficiality of busy church schedules to find moments of true spiritual unity.

- **Impact on Marital Health (Malachi 2:14)**
  A strong spiritual foundation positively impacts all areas of a marriage, from enhancing emotional intimacy to reinforcing mutual respect. It provides couples with the resilience to face challenges, drawing strength from their faith and each other.

- **The Danger of Spiritual Neglect (Matthew 18:19-20)**
  Neglecting the spiritual aspect of a marriage can lead to a sense of emptiness and disconnection, undermining the relationship's foundation. Recognizing and addressing this neglect is crucial for the overall health and vitality of the marriage.

- **The Role of Shared Faith Experiences (Song of Solomon 8:6)**

Engaging in shared faith experiences strengthens the marital bond and aligns the couple with God's purpose for their union. This shared spiritual journey enriches the marriage, offering deeper meaning and fulfillment in everyday life.

🪶 Personal Reflection

Consider the routines and rituals in your marriage. Have any spiritual practices become more routine than meaningful? Confess where purpose has been lost, and think of one way to renew intimacy and connection in these areas.

_____
_____
_____
_____
_____
_____
_____
_____
_____

💍 Couple's Discussion

Recall the last time you both felt a deep spiritual connection—whether through prayer, worship, or a shared faith experience. Share how it impacted your relationship and confess any challenges in making these moments consistent. Talk about practical ways to cultivate more of these experiences, strengthening your spiritual bond and unity in Christ.

Day 52: Ritual of Connection

And now these three remain: faith, hope and love. But the greatest of these is love.

1 Corinthians 13:13

Spiritual fidelity is rooted in love—the greatest gift and the ultimate bond of faith and hope within a marriage. This love is seen in acts of kindness, support, and shared prayer, weaving your spirits together in God's grace. As you explore spiritual fidelity, reflect on God's vast love for you and your spouse, and strive to mirror that love in your relationship.

This love can transform, heal, and unite, drawing you closer to each other and to God. Spiritual fidelity goes beyond religious practices; it is about living out Christ's love—a love so profound it becomes the foundation of your marriage.

Let this love guide your actions, strengthen your bond, and deepen your connection with God and each other. In embodying this love, your marriage becomes a testament to the power of God's grace and faithfulness.

Daily Prayer

Heavenly Father,

We come before You with grateful hearts, thankful for the journey of spiritual fidelity You've guided us on. Teach us to love as You love, with patience, kindness, and forgiveness. Let Your love be the anchor of our marriage, guiding us through challenges and celebrating with us in joy. Help us to see each other through Your eyes, recognizing the divine spark within each other. As we continue to grow in our faith together, let our love reflect Your own, creating a testament to the power and beauty of a life lived in harmony with You.

Amen.

Fidelity Builder: Private Worship and Service Night

Objective

This activity aims to deepen your spiritual connection and reinforce the principles of humility, service, and love within your marriage. By engaging in worship and the symbolic act of washing each other's feet, you embody the love and humility Christ showed us.

Instructions

1. **Preparation**
   - Set aside a specific evening for this activity.
   - Prepare a comfortable space in your home where you can worship together without distractions. This can be your living room, a backyard, or any place that feels peaceful.
   - Gather necessary items: a basin, warm water, towels, and comfortable seating.
   - Choose worship songs that are meaningful to both of you. This could include a mix of hymns, contemporary Christian music, or instrumental pieces conducive to reflection and prayer.

2. **Worship**
   - Begin the evening by praying together, inviting God's presence into your time of worship.
   - Play the worship music you have selected. Sing together, or if singing is not comfortable for you, simply listen and reflect on the lyrics.

3. **Foot Washing Ceremony**
   - Transition from worship to the foot washing ceremony. Explain to each other why you chose this act, focusing on its symbolism of service, humility, and love.
   - Read John 13 together.
   - One partner at a time, gently wash each other's feet in the basin. As you do this, pray for your spouse, asking God to bless them, to guide them, and to protect your marriage.
   - After washing, dry each other's feet with the towels.

4. **Closing:**
   - Conclude the activity with a prayer together, thanking God for the gift of your spouse and the journey of marriage you share.
   - Share any thoughts or feelings that arose during the worship and foot washing. Discuss how you can carry the humility and service demonstrated into your daily lives as a couple.

Reflection

This activity is not just about the acts of worship and service; it is a powerful reminder of the depth of love and commitment you share. It is an opportunity to express love in a profoundly humble and Christ-like manner, strengthening the spiritual and emotional bonds of your marriage.

Day 53: Refocusing Faith

For the Lord your God is the one who goes with you to fight for you against your enemies to give you victory.

Deuteronomy 20:4

In every marriage, there exists an unseen battleground where the integrity and depth of the relationship are constantly tested. This battleground is not of the world we see but is deeply rooted in the spiritual realm, where the true essence of our connections and our faithfulness to each other and to God are challenged. The story of a couple, deeply committed to their faith and ministry, serves as a poignant illustration of how easily the fabric of marriage can unravel when spiritual intimacy is overlooked. Their journey from being models of Christian service to confronting a crisis that threatened the very foundation of their marriage highlights the critical need for spiritual fidelity.

As this couple discovered, the vigor of serving in various ministries could not compensate for the growing spiritual void within their home. Their once vibrant shared spiritual life had become overshadowed by a relentless pursuit of communal spiritual accolades, leaving their personal connection with God and each other as mere afterthoughts. The turning point came when they recognized that their overwhelming involvement in external church activities had masked a profound spiritual disconnect. This realization sparked a journey towards rekindling their spiritual oneness, emphasizing that true ministry begins within the sanctity of the marital relationship.

📖 Daily Prayer

Lord,

Help us to recognize the sacredness of our spiritual journey together as a couple. Teach us to prioritize our spiritual connection, ensuring that it remains the cornerstone of our marriage. Guide us in finding joy in the simplicity of shared prayer, study, and worship. Let our love for You be the bond that strengthens our love for each other, transforming every aspect of our marriage into a testament of Your grace and faithfulness.

In Jesus' Name, Amen.

📖 Read: Chapter 14, Pages 337-341

The reading for today underscores the delicate nature of marital harmony, emphasizing that neglecting spiritual intimacy can lead to profound disconnection, even in outwardly active religious lives. It highlights the journey of reevaluating priorities and rediscovering the essence of spiritual togetherness, advocating for a deliberate recommitment to shared spiritual practices. Through a thoughtful process of re-engagement with faith, the story illustrates how couples can navigate through periods of spiritual drought, reviving the foundational aspects of their relationship that initially brought them together.

🔑 Key Points

- **Foundation of Spiritual Intimacy (1 John 4:12)**

    A genuine spiritual connection in a marriage transcends routine religious activities, fostering a profound bond that not only draws partners closer to each other but also deepens their relationship with God. This kind of intimacy transforms everyday interactions into meaningful experiences, strengthening the marriage.

- **Revitalizing Shared Spiritual Paths (Malachi 2:15)**

    For a marriage to flourish spiritually, it is essential for partners to intentionally direct their attention to their collective journey in faith. This commitment might involve carving out dedicated moments for joint prayer and engaging in Bible study, stepping away from the whirlwind of structured religious events to foster genuine spiritual connections.

- **Influence on Marital Dynamics (Proverbs 3:3-4)**

    A robust spiritual foundation positively influences all facets of a marriage, enhancing emotional intimacy, fostering respect, and providing a resilient framework to withstand life's challenges. It equips couples with spiritual and emotional resources to support each other more effectively.

- **Consequences of Spiritual Neglect (Hosea 4:6)**

    Ignoring the spiritual dimension of marriage can lead to a void of intimacy and connection, undermining the partnership's stability. Recognizing and addressing this neglect is essential for the health and vitality of the relationship, requiring a shift in focus back to foundational spiritual practices.

- **Shared Faith Experiences (Deuteronomy 6:6-7)**

Actively engaging in shared faith experiences, such as worship, ministry, and community service, not only strengthens the marital bond but also aligns the couple with God's vision for their union. These activities reinforce the couple's commitment to each other and their faith, enriching their marriage with deeper significance and fulfillment.

Personal Reflection

Recall the last meaningful spiritual conversation or prayer you shared with your spouse. How frequent are these moments? Confess any barriers preventing deeper spiritual engagement and identify one step to enhance your shared spiritual journey.

_____
_____
_____
_____
_____
_____
_____
_____
_____

Couple's Discussion

Talk about how busyness and outside commitments have impacted your spiritual growth as a couple. Confess any ways you may have neglected your shared spiritual health and how it has affected your relationship. Discuss how you can intentionally prioritize spiritual connection moving forward through practices like prayer, Bible study, and honest conversations, ensuring that your faith remains central in your marriage.

Day 54: Full Armor of God

Put on the full armor of God, so that you can take your stand against the devil's schemes.

Ephesians 6:11

Spiritual fidelity in marriage requires donning the full armor of God. It is a deliberate act of fortifying the relationship against trials and adversities. This spiritual armor encompasses truth, righteousness, readiness from the gospel of peace, faith, salvation, and the Word of God. Just as the armor protects a soldier in battle, spiritual fidelity safeguards the sacred covenant of marriage.

Regular engagement in prayer and Bible study acts as the belt of truth and the breastplate of righteousness, establishing a firm foundation in God's truth. Participating in church, serving together, and engaging in couples' Bible study are ways to fit your feet with readiness and lift the shield of faith. These activities not only draw couples closer to God but also to each other, reinforcing their union with layers of divine strength and wisdom.

Praying for and with each other is the helmet of salvation in action, a critical defense against despair and disconnection. Setting spiritual goals and celebrating religious milestones together wields the sword of the Spirit, cutting through challenges and deepening the marital bond.

Daily Prayer

Heavenly Father,

We come before You today to ask for Your guidance and protection over our marriage. Help us to put on the full armor of God every day so that we can stand strong against any challenge that comes our way. May our relationship be grounded in Your truth, righteousness, and peace. Give us the courage to face each day with faith, the hope of salvation, and the wisdom of Your Word. Let our love for each other be a reflection of Your love for us.

In Jesus' Name, we pray, Amen.

Read: Chapter 14, Pages 341-347

In the context of a marriage strengthened by spiritual fidelity, likened to wearing the full armor of God, couples are equipped to face both internal and external challenges with unwavering hope, strength, and love. This spiritual readiness involves regular Bible study, prayer, active church participation, and shared faith experiences, acting as the foundational layers of truth, righteousness, readiness from the gospel, faith, salvation, and the Word of God. Through these practices, partners reinforce their bond and commitment, ensuring their relationship can withstand and thrive amidst life's trials, thereby maintaining a resilient and faithful union reflective of their dedication to God and each other.

🔑 Key Points

- **Foundational Practices (2 Timothy 3:16-17)**
  Bible study and prayer serve as the core practices for couples seeking to enhance their spiritual connection, symbolizing the belt of truth and breastplate of righteousness. These activities ground the relationship in Christ's teachings, offering guidance and a deeper bond with God and each other.

- **Church and Ministry Participation (Hebrews 10:24-25)**
  Engaging in church services and ministry work together acts as a means of reinforcing the couple's bond and providing them with a shared sense of purpose. This involvement is likened to having feet fitted with the readiness from the gospel of peace, preparing them to face life's challenges with a united front and a supportive community.

- **Couples' Bible Study and Community (Proverbs 27:17)**
  Joining a couples' Bible study group or a faith community equips couples with the shield of faith, protecting them from doubts and conflicts. It offers a platform for mutual spiritual growth and understanding, fostering a stronger relationship and deeper empathy between partners.

- **Prayer and Spiritual Support (1 Thessalonians 5:11)**
  Praying together and for each other strengthens the couple's spiritual intimacy, symbolized by the helmet of salvation. It encourages emotional and spiritual support, particularly through challenging times, reinforcing their love and commitment to each other.

- **Shared Spiritual Goals and Celebrations (Joshua 24:15)**
  Setting spiritual goals and celebrating religious milestones together wields the sword of the Spirit in the marriage. These shared acts of faithfulness serve as reminders of God's presence and faithfulness, providing strength, renewal, and a deeper sense of unity within the marriage.

Personal Reflection

Consider your commitment to daily spiritual practices. How are you embodying the full armor of God in your life? Confess any areas where you may lack consistency, and identify one step to strengthen your spiritual resilience.

___

___

___

___

___

___

___

___

___

Couple's Discussion

Discuss how you can put on the full armor of God together to protect and strengthen your marriage. Confess any areas where you have struggled to remain spiritually guarded or have neglected shared spiritual practices. Identify specific actions—such as Bible study, prayer, or faith-based activities—that can help you grow in unity, deepen your faith, and ensure your marriage reflects God's love and purpose.

Day 55: Harmony In Marriage

*How good and pleasant it is
when God's people live together in unity!*

Psalm 133:1

Harmony in Marriage mirrors the intricate and beautiful harmony found in music, where diverse notes blend to create a more profound, unified sound. This divine orchestration reflects the unity within the Trinity—Father, Son, and Holy Spirit—each distinct yet perfectly united, serving as a model for marital relationships. In a harmonious marriage, differences are not merely tolerated but celebrated as complementary, each spouse's unique qualities enhancing the unity and purpose of their partnership.

This unity is not a product of sameness but a testament to the strength found in diversity, bound by love and mutual submission. As each spouse engages in their God-given roles, supports each other's spiritual growth, and navigates life's challenges together, their marriage becomes a reflection of God's unity, love, and sacrificial nature. The goal of such harmony is not just personal happiness but glorifying God through a testament of love, unity, and fidelity that mirrors the perfect harmony of the Trinity.

📖 Daily Prayer

Heavenly Father,

We come before You to thank You for the gift of marriage and the beautiful example of perfect unity found in the Trinity. Help us to embody this divine harmony in our marriage, celebrating our differences as strengths that, when united, reflect Your love and glory. Teach us to navigate our challenges together, with love, patience, and understanding, always aiming to glorify You through the fidelity and unity of our bond. May our marriage be a testament to the beauty of Your design, a melody of hope, influence, and fidelity that sings of Your faithfulness and love.

Amen.

📖 Read: Part 4 Introduction, Pages 348-351

Our final day of reading explores the intricate parallels between musical harmony and the unity found in marriage, emphasizing that such harmony is not merely the sum of its parts but a divine orchestration of diverse elements leading to a more profound, enriching experience. This harmony is likened to the relationship between Christ and the church, reflecting a deep, meaningful alignment of lives guided by divine love and wisdom. The ultimate model for this unity is the Trinity—Father, Son, and Holy Spirit—whose perfect love, mutual submission, and seamless cooperation provide an exemplary blueprint for marital harmony. This concept extends beyond mere coexistence, suggesting that each spouse, while retaining individuality, contributes to a unified whole that glorifies God, showcasing a relationship built on selfless love, mutual respect, and complementary roles.

🔑 Key Points

- **Trinitarian Model for Marital Harmony (John 17:20-23)**
  The Trinity exemplifies perfect unity in diversity, serving as a profound model for marriage. In a harmonious marriage, spouses maintain their distinct identities yet work together in unity, mirroring the relationship within the Godhead. This divine example underscores the importance of love, respect, and mutual submission in cultivating a harmonious marital relationship.

- **Foundational Elements of Harmony (1 Corinthians 13:4-7)**
  The text highlights hope, influence, and fidelity as foundational to achieving harmony in marriage. These elements, drawn from biblical teachings, form the basis for a relationship that is both enriching and stable, navigating life's challenges with grace and strengthening the marital bond through shared spiritual growth and commitment.

- **Challenges to Harmony (Proverbs 15:1)**
  Identifying potential threats such as unresolved conflicts, financial strains, and infidelity is crucial for maintaining harmony. The text emphasizes the importance of communication and godly responses to conflicts, suggesting that daily interactions and attitudes play a significant role in either fostering harmony or sowing discord within the marriage.

- **Achieving Harmony through Shared Practices (Colossians 3:16)**
  Engaging in joint spiritual practices like Bible study and prayer is highlighted as essential for deepening the connection between spouses. These practices not only bring couples closer to God but also to each other, reinforcing their bond through shared experiences and mutual support.

- **Marriage as Discipleship (1 Peter 3:1-2)**

  The text posits marriage as an avenue for discipleship, encouraging couples to view their relationship as a ministry. This perspective invites couples to share the harmony they have cultivated with others, extending the principles of their unity to serve as a model for godly relationships within their community.

Personal Reflection

Think about the unique parts of your personality and how they contribute to your marriage. How do your individual strengths help bring balance and harmony to your relationship? Identify one strength your spouse has that you do not, and confess whether you admire it, feel intimidated by it, or have even envied it. Consider how you can embrace and appreciate this difference to grow together.

_____
_____
_____
_____
_____
_____
_____
_____

Couple's Discussion

Reflect on how hope, influence, and fidelity are lived out in your marriage. Confess any struggles in fully embracing these principles and how they have impacted your relationship. Share specific moments where leaning on these foundations helped you navigate challenges together. Discuss ways you can further strengthen your bond by embodying the unity and love reflected in the Trinity.

Harmony In Marriage: Couple's Workbook

Day 56: I Do

Because of the Lord's great love we are not consumed,
for his compassions never fail.
²³ They are new every morning;
great is your faithfulness.

Lamentations 3:22-23

In the glow of a wedding day, when the words "I do" are exchanged, they shine with the promise of a lifetime. Yet, these vows, potent with commitment and hope, are not meant to be spoken once but lived out daily. Lamentations 3:22-23 reminds us of God's steadfast love and mercy that are new every morning; similarly, our commitment to our spouse—a reflection of divine constancy—requires daily renewal.

Each morning, as we first encounter our partner (with bed hair and morning breath), let it be with a heart that says "I do" once again. This daily affirmation transcends the routine of life, grounding our relationship in a love that mirrors the unfailing nature of God's love for us. It is in the daily choosing, beyond the realm of feelings and circumstances, that the depth of our vows is truly measured.

Our partner's "I do" is a gift of trust, an assurance of mutual commitment. Recognizing this, let us strive to honor and cherish it with every action, word, and thought. This continual choice to love and serve each other in Christ creates a marriage that not only stands the test of time but also reflects the kingdom of God in its truest form.

📖 Daily Prayer

Heavenly Father,

As we wake each day, let our first thought be a renewal of our vow to love and serve our spouse. Remind us that "I do" is not just a promise made in the past, but a declaration lived out in every moment of our shared life. Help us to cherish and honor this commitment, seeing in our partner's eyes the same love and dedication. May our marriage be a testament to Your unfailing love and faithfulness, today and every day.

In Jesus' precious name, Amen.

✒ Personal Reflection

Over the past eight weeks, which area of fidelity (Experiential, Intellectual, Emotional, Financial, Sexual, Spiritual) has shown the most growth in your life? Which has been the most challenging? Confess any struggles you have faced and reflect on how these challenges and victories have shaped your perspective on harmony in your marriage.

_____
_____
_____
_____
_____
_____
_____
_____
_____
_____
_____
_____
_____
_____
_____

⚭ Couple's Discussion

As you reflect on this eight-week journey, share how your understanding of hope, influence, and the six fidelities has shaped your vision of harmony in your marriage. Confess any past struggles in fully embracing these principles and acknowledge the growth you've seen in each other. Discuss how you can daily renew your vows—both in spirit and action—to continue nurturing intimacy, trust, and unity in your relationship.

What's Next?

As you near the end of this part of our journey with *Harmony In Marriage*, it is essential to consider the steps ahead on this shared path of spiritual growth and commitment. Your exploration of the intricate merging of two souls in unity with Christ, grounded in divine love, sets a foundation for what comes next: extending the fruits of your harmony beyond the confines of your relationship.

The journey does not end here; it is a continuous process of learning, growing, and sharing. Much like discipleship, the essence of a harmonious marriage is about reflecting Christ's love to each other and the world. This reflection can manifest in various forms, including engaging in ministry together or serving as mentors to other couples. Embracing these roles allows you to practice the principles you have learned, deepening your relationship with God and each other while impacting your community positively.

However, the pursuit of harmony may reveal areas within your relationship that require further attention or healing. It is natural; no marriage is without its challenges. If certain aspects of fidelity—be it emotional, intellectual, financial, sexual, or spiritual—pose continual obstacles to your marital unity, seeking deeper group support or biblical couples counseling could be invaluable. These resources offer a safe space to explore vulnerabilities, heal wounds, and fortify your bond, underpinned by godly wisdom and compassion.

Consider joining a marriage enrichment group within your church community or participating in workshops that focus on strengthening marital bonds. Such engagements provide not only practical tools and insights for nurturing your relationship but also the fellowship of like-minded couples. This communal aspect can be particularly enriching, reminding you that you are not alone in your journey towards a more profound harmony.

In the spirit of discipleship, remember that your marriage is a powerful testimony of God's grace and love. As you continue to build on the harmony you have cultivated, let your relationship be a source of inspiration and guidance for others. Sharing your experiences, challenges, and victories can be a ministry, offering hope and encouragement to couples at different stages of their journey.

Finally, always keep the lines of communication open between you and your partner, and with God at the center of your relationship. Pray together, seeking His guidance and wisdom as you step into the next phase of your marital journey. May your marriage continue to grow in love and grace, reflecting the beauty of God's design for union and harmony.

About The Ministry

The Encounter Ministry serves as the educational and discipleship beacon of Men of Purpose LLC, a dedicated 501(c)3 non-profit initiative. The heartbeat of our ministry lies in a simple yet profound vision: to ensure that both men and women are deeply rooted and well-equipped in the ministry of the Word, enabling them to be guiding lights within their families, pillars in their churches, and influential leaders in their communities.

For over a decade, we have been unwavering in our commitment. Our weekend Encounters have become cherished getaways, offering deep spiritual rejuvenation, while our weekly discipleship programs for men and women have been catalysts for personal growth and communal bonding.

Recognizing the foundation of society in strong, united families, we have taken a great and meaningful step forward. We are ardently answering our call to mentor and guide married couples, assisting them in weaving relationships that mirror the beauty and strength of biblical marriages. In all our endeavors, one principle remains clear and unshaken: the centrality of Christ. By emphasizing His teachings and His love, we aim to anchor every facet of our lives, particularly our families, in Christ's unwavering love.

About The Author

Rob Rodriguez serves passionately as a biblical counselor with Encounter Ministry. He has walked alongside countless individuals and couples on their transformative spiritual journeys for over fifteen years. With every life Jesus touches, Rob remains inspired by the remarkable transformations God enacts in those who ask. He also shares his insights and passion for teaching as an adjunct professor in the Practical Psychology department at Multnomah University.

Based in Northern Nevada, Rob cherishes every moment with his close family of three loving daughters, an awesome bonus son, and an amazing grandson. He began his academic journey with a bachelor's in counseling psychology from William Jessup University. Continuing his education, Rob has completed two master's degrees, including an M.A. in Pastoral Counseling and a Master of Divinity from Liberty University. He is now pursuing a Doctor of Ministry in Biblical Counseling at Southwestern Baptist Theological Seminary, developing a program for training lay church leaders in biblical counseling. Through his ministry, Rob aims to be a part of the discipleship and equipping of all who feel called into the ministry of soul care.

Made in the USA
Las Vegas, NV
07 March 2025